KEEPING IT CIVIL

Keeping It Civil

The Case of the Pre-nup
and the Porsche
& Other True Accounts
from the Files of a
Family Lawyer

Margaret Klaw

ALGONQUIN BOOKS OF CHAPEL HILL   2013

Published by
ALGONQUIN BOOKS OF CHAPEL HILL
Post Office Box 2225
Chapel Hill, North Carolina 27515-2225

a division of
WORKMAN PUBLISHING
225 Varick Street
New York, New York 10014

Printed in the United States of America.
Published simultaneously in Canada by Thomas Allen & Son Limited.
Design by Anne Winslow.

Library of Congress Cataloging-in-Publication Data
Klaw, Margaret, [date]
   Keeping it civil : the case of the pre-nup and the Porsche and other true
accounts from the files of a family lawyer.—First Edition.
      pages cm
   ISBN 978-1-61620-239-2
   1. Klaw, Margaret, [date]   2. Lawyers—Pennsylvania—
Philadelphia—Biography.   3. Domestic relations—
Pennsylvania—Philadelphia.   I. Title.
   KF373.K53A3 2013
   346.74801'5092—dc23   2013014925

10 9 8 7 6 5 4 3 2 1
First Edition

To Alan and Joni,
my partners in life and in law

Contents

KEEPING IT CIVIL

Opening Statement

I'm a family law junkie. I am riveted by the vor-
tex of marriage, divorce, parenthood, sex, money,
love, anger, betrayal, sexual orientation, reproductive technology, and the rapidly shifting legal landscape on which it
all plays out. Family law issues are debated and dissected
everywhere we turn, from the hair salon to the state supreme court, because they affect us all, directly or indirectly.
They go to the very core of who we are, to our most intimate selves. And to the intimate selves of our neighbors. We
are, let's face it, endlessly fascinated by how other people
live, love, and often screw up their lives.

Family law is also on the cutting edge of our changing
cultural norms, as society wrestles with the expanding definition of family. Same-sex marriage, open adoption, gay and
lesbian couples raising their biological or adopted children,
reproductive technology that spreads out the components
of parenthood among multiple people (intended parents,
egg donors, sperm donors, gestational carriers)—as these

new configurations emerge, old boundaries dissolve. I work in the trenches of this rapidly morphing world, but I find myself frequently frustrated that I don't have more time to reflect on it. A day at my busy Philadelphia law firm can become just a series of emails and phone calls and letters and meetings, punctuated by billing each task in tenths of an hour, a string of individual activities stretching out like a river behind and ahead of me with no resting spot. Each case can be broken up into so many little fragments that the big picture recedes.

The chapters that follow are the result of precious moments stolen away from that long march of the billable hour. They are not meant to be a comprehensive overview of the practice of family law or a how-to guide to navigating the legal system. My intention was simply to write about my own experiences practicing law and building a law firm over the last twenty-five years, to provide snapshots of specific moments in time, a chronicle of events legal and social, pulled from hectic days in court, in the office, and, occasionally, at the dining room table. With the exception of the chapters titled "Anatomy of a Trial," which run throughout the book and are a composite based on many custody cases I have tried, all the cases and clients I write about are real. I have, of course, changed names and identifying details to protect privacy and client confidentiality where necessary.

Family law can be messy and complicated and frustrating, but to me it is always exhilarating, characterized by high drama and powerful emotion. As we divorce lawyers often say, whether in rueful punctuation at the end of difficult phone calls with opposing counsel or in the course of bemused *tsk-tsk*ing while sipping cocktails at bar association receptions, *You couldn't make this stuff up, right?* Our colleague, nodding his or her head emphatically, will reply *No, you certainly could not.*

And then one of us will laugh and say *Someday, I've got to write a book about it.*

The Wall

Darlene was a pretty, blond nineteen-year-old with a ten-month-old baby girl whom she wheeled into my office in a ragged umbrella stroller. Darlene, the baby, and the baby's father, Keith, had been living with Keith's parents in a row house in northeast Philly. Keith and Darlene apparently argued a lot, and one day, during a fight about Darlene's wanting Keith to watch the baby so she could go out with her girlfriends, Keith put his hands around Darlene's neck and tried to choke her. Darlene had filed in court for and received a protection order to keep Keith away from her and the baby. Keith, in response, had turned around and filed for custody of the baby, alleging that Darlene was a drug addict.

At this time I was about five years out of law school and working for a nonprofit legal center. Darlene's was one of my first custody cases. Like Darlene, I had a ten-month-old daughter. I worked three days a week and stayed home with my baby and four-year-old the rest of the time. I was still immersed in that mothering cocoon that descended upon me after the birth of each of my daughters, venturing out to do battle in a world of conflict and aggression that was my legal life and retreating back into the sweet, cozy routine of trips to story hour at the library and long afternoons of play groups and coffee with my friends and their babies.

Darlene's case really got to me. Her baby became my baby in my mind as I transitioned between my two worlds. I felt pure outrage that this abusive young thug was trying to take a precious little baby away from her mother—my client!—and incredible fear that it could happen on my watch. I felt sick as a mother and terrified as a professional, and I wasn't sure which was which.

Darlene and I met at the courthouse on the day of the custody hearing. She was wearing extremely tight blue jeans, which annoyed me because I wanted her to look like Madonna (not the singer, the other one) but then decided that it was my fault for neglecting to prep her on what to wear to court—and, anyway, there was no point in bringing it up because it was too late to do anything about it. I focused on finding the courtroom without looking like an idiot. I had not handled many cases in Philadelphia, and I desperately did not want Darlene to know I had no idea where I was going. Somehow, I managed to find the right door without asking anyone and totally blowing my cover.

We walked into an ancient, crumbling courtroom with dusty portraits of dead judges on the walls, high ceilings, and stains on the polished marble floors—faded elegance from another era, turned shabby and depressing. The judge was old and white haired and imposing, peering down at us from the bench. I had never appeared before him and had no idea what to expect, an unnerving situation in any case. Keith was there, looking like a choir boy with tattoos. His parents were also present, looking kindly, sensible, and grandparental, although probably considerably younger than I am as I write this.

The proceeding itself is a blur. I remember only a conference in chambers—close, dark, intimate, but extremely formal—where I struggled to get the judge to understand the retaliatory nature of Keith's request for custody and his history of physically abusing Darlene, which included a number of assaults prior to the recent choking incident. There must have been witnesses called and testimony taken, but all that has been eclipsed by the stunning clarity with which I recall the outcome of the case and its aftermath: His Honor decided to take the baby away from both of them and award custody to Keith's parents. The legal basis on which he did so eluded me then and eludes me still, as the grandparents never even asked for custody, but nonetheless that's what happened.

When the ruling was announced, Darlene was, literally, hysterical. I dragged her out of the courtroom into a long and dingy hallway, where she dropped violently to the floor, curled up in the fetal position, and began to rock back and forth, wailing "She's my baby, I had her, I have the stretch marks to prove it, she's my baby, how can he take her away from me?" The uniformed court officers in the hallway looked on helplessly, and I felt like I was going to throw up.

That was a Friday afternoon. I went home and looked at my baby and started to cry. I felt physical pain everywhere in my body. I completely understood why Darlene was rolling on the floor of the courthouse, showing her stretch marks to the court officers. The thought of the state's removing my little Robin and giving her to someone else to raise was intolerable. Over and over again, I told my husband about what happened, looking for reassurance that it wasn't my fault, something he couldn't tell me with any credibility whatsoever since he (a) wasn't there, and (b) wasn't a lawyer and had absolutely no idea what I should or shouldn't have done, and (c) generally tells me he's sure I did a great job anyway. I dreaded the next week when I was going to have to be the lawyer, when I was going to have to talk to Darlene and figure out a strategy for reclaiming the baby. I was the grown-up, the professional, and I had screwed up royally.

Monday, back in the office, Darlene called. I launched into the speech I had prepared, explaining my recommendation that we immediately file a petition for reconsideration of the judge's order. She interrupted me with a perky, "Oh, that's okay—I'm engaged!" and proceeded to tell me that she and Keith had patched it all up and everything was great and he had given her a ring and she was back living with him and his parents and their daughter, all together, one big happy family. What a difference forty-eight hours had made. She thanked me for my help and hung up.

I was stunned. Then I got angry. First I was angry at Darlene for being so immature and deciding to marry this abusive guy who tried to choke her to death and to take her baby away by lying about her being a drug addict, just because he said he was sorry and bought her a ring. A ring! Then my anger turned to fury as I started feeling sorry for myself. Didn't she know what she put me through? Didn't she know how much I cared? Didn't she know how I had cried when I looked at my baby and thought of hers? Most important, of course, didn't she know she had totally ruined my weekend?

LAWYERS EITHER LOVE or hate family law. Very few are neutral about it. When I tell a fellow member of the bar what area of law I practice, I frequently get a groan in response. Usually that lawyer says he handled one divorce case and "never again." I will be the first to admit that the intersection—collision, often—of family life and the law is daunting to navigate. People are in various stages of crisis, and the available legal remedies are frequently inadequate. It's easy to feel ineffective and it's common to have unhappy clients. But the opposite side of that coin is that when you can fix a problem, when the outcome is good, it's incredibly satisfying. You are invested in your clients because the issues they are struggling with—children, marriage, sexual orientation, personal finance—are so important and you come to know them so well. And yes, at some level, you identify with them. That's what makes the lawyer at the cocktail party groan. But it's also what makes my partner call me, as I'm sitting in my living room typing these words, so excited to tell me about a psychologist's report we just received that backs up what our client told us about her ex-husband's abuse of their children, which means his access to them will in all likelihood be limited by the judge, which means we are going to be able to protect her kids, which means we are really doing something valuable.

The identification-with-the-client thing is rough. And nowhere is it rougher than in a custody case, especially, I suspect, if you have children yourself; witness my response to Darlene. You have to find the right balance between caring about the outcome of the case and putting some kind of wall between you and your client so you can continue to live your life without internalizing the client's problems. After Darlene's case, something shifted inside me and the wall started to go up. I realized that Darlene had managed her life for nineteen years without any input from me. She came to me in a time of crisis to help her with a specific problem, and I did my best. But her baby girl wasn't Robin and her stretch marks weren't mine.

Now that I've been doing this for decades, my wall is more firmly in place. However, some cases still cause me angst, and high on the list are those that involve a parent who wants to relocate with his or her kids. Most custody cases present conflicts in which compromise is always a possibility, because there is middle ground to explore, an extra overnight on alternate weeks, a visit for dinner but not overnight. A relocation case is a different animal entirely. If a parent wants to move from Connecticut to California and take her kids with her, there is no compromise: The kids either go or stay; you cannot split the baby. The stakes are high, the law is murky, and regardless of the outcome, one parent is going to suffer tremendously.

Not too long ago, I represented a woman who wanted to relocate to Atlanta with her ten-year-old son and six-year-old daughter. Susan was a graphic artist who had married an academic, something of a rock star in his field. When their son was a toddler, they had moved to Philadelphia from Atlanta, where they were both raised. He'd been offered a tenured position as head of the department. Susan settled in, and their daughter was born a couple of years later. She never liked Philadelphia, and her husband always promised her they would eventually move back home. Then their marriage soured and they separated. They shared custody of their children pretty equally in terms of time, but

Susan, who worked from home and had a flexible schedule, did much more of the day-to-day stuff, the doctor's appointments, school projects, Halloween costumes.

When they had been living apart for a while but had still not divorced, Susan became involved with her high school boyfriend. Divorced, he lived in Atlanta and had custody of his twelve-year-old daughter. When he and Susan became engaged, I began negotiating with her husband's lawyer. Would he agree to allow her to relocate to Atlanta with the children if he could have them with him in the summers, for school vacations, and whenever he was in Atlanta visiting his relatives? He wouldn't, so we had to go forward with a custody trial to determine whether Susan would be allowed to take the children to Georgia to live with her and her fiancé (whom she planned to marry the minute the divorce became final). There was a particular urgency to this, because Susan and her fiancé wanted to have children together and they wanted to do it soon, as Susan was already in her forties.

As it turned out, they decided not to wait. By the time our court date rolled around, Susan was pregnant. So the stakes had been raised again. If the judge denied her request to relocate the children, she was not going to go without them. She would have to stay in Philadelphia and give birth to the baby alone, with her fiancé visiting when he could.

In cases involving relocation in Pennsylvania, and in many other jurisdictions, the judge has to find that the advantages to the children of the proposed move outweigh the detriment to them of seeing the staying-behind parent less frequently. These kids saw their father a lot and had a close relationship with him, so this was a hard burden to meet.

The trial lasted for three days and included a number of witnesses in addition to Susan, her husband, and her fiancé. We presented testimony about the great schools the kids would attend in Atlanta versus their not-so-great schools in Philly, the proximity they would have to extended family on both sides, all of whom lived in the Atlanta area, and the advantages of the more relaxed, outdoor lifestyle they would lead in the community where Susan planned to live. Susan testified about the better employment opportunities for graphic artists in the less saturated market and the importance of having her family as a support network for her and the children.

The judge also interviewed the children in her chambers, taking off her black robe, relaxing them with candy and chit-chat, and asking them directly how they would feel about moving to Atlanta with their mother. The elephant in the courtroom was really the issue of the pregnancy and the new relationship. How could the judge ask Susan, who moved to Philadelphia solely to support the career of the man she was divorcing, to forgo the new life she wanted to make for herself with remarriage and children? On other hand, how could the judge ask Susan's husband to forgo being part of his children's school year—no coaching the base-ball team; no school concerts; no casual, daily parenting—because his soon-to-be-ex-wife decided to get pregnant and engaged to someone who lived in Atlanta? While I desperately wanted to win the case for Susan, I would not have wanted to be the judge.

The trial went well but the judge did not issue an order from the bench. She took the case "under advisement," meaning she needed to think about it. It was nerve racking for Susan, who had to lay all the groundwork in Atlanta for the move, such as enrollment in new schools, finding a house to live in with her fiancé and their expanding family, and planning the logistics of the move from Philadelphia, but could commit to none of it, since it all hinged on the judge's ruling.

The two weeks or so we waited for a decision seemed endless. I was having dreams about the case, dreams in which Susan was giving birth to multiple new children, dreams in which I needed to appear for additional days of trial but didn't know when they were scheduled, dreams in which I was moving to Atlanta, too. Finally, the fax machine screeched (faxing remains the Philadelphia family court's preferred method of communication) and I read the judge's order as it slowly rolled out. I remember screaming. She ruled in our favor. The children were permitted to relocate with Susan to Atlanta that summer. Susan was ecstatic and grateful, and of course, I let myself feel like the hero. I still have a little card taped to my computer moni-tor that came with the flowers Susan's fiancé sent me. It simply says "thank you thank you thank you thank you." Susan and the children moved, the baby (a girl) was born in Atlanta, the divorce became final, and she and her fiancé were married.

When you have a big victory like this, the wall doesn't matter so much; in fact, the lower the wall is, the higher the high is and the better the celebratory drink tastes. But I know I need to keep it in check. It's kind of like hedging your bets in the stock market—you win some and you lose some, so you need to be prepared. No more post-Darlene-rolling-on-the-courthouse-floor weekends.

WHILE RELOCATION CASES are high-stakes, win-lose scenarios, there is another type of case that also causes the wall to crumble. It's the case in which an injustice was done before my involvement and my job is to try to undo it. There is nothing that gets a lawyer more fired up—and this cuts across all areas of legal practice—than a govern-ment agency screwing somebody when the law provides a clear remedy. And of course, in the context of custody, this usually means that a parent can't be with his or her child, which is heart-wrenching.

Eric was a sweet, young, soft-spoken, dreadlocked, new-agey kind of dad who played keyboards in a band and had four-and-a-half-year-old twin boys with a woman from whom he'd been separated since the twins were infants. At the time he first came to my office he hadn't seen them in about ten months. He was despondent.

One day, out of the blue, he had received a call from a social worker who said she needed to talk to him about a report of child abuse regarding his children. He met with the social worker, who asked him lots of questions about his activities with the boys in recent days. She also interviewed the mother and the children, who were then about three and a half. She instructed Eric that he was not allowed to have any contact with the boys while the investigation was pending. The social worker would not tell him what he had allegedly done, and the children's mother refused to talk to him at all. Eric had no idea what was going on. He was young and not very sophisticated and he assumed, as many people would, that he had to do what the social worker dictated or he could be arrested. He hoped things would blow over with the twins' mother and she would let him start seeing his kids again.

When Eric finally sought counsel, I was quickly able to determine that, despite what the social worker had said, there was no court order restricting his access to the children. Unfortunately, this is a common occurrence in cases that involve the intersection between child protective services (agencies charged with investigating and handling child abuse cases) and custody (disputes between parents). It amounts to a total lack of due process. There is no notice of the allegations, no opportunity to address them. Since there was no order from the court that hears child abuse cases, and since the mother's refusal to allow Eric to see the children was based solely on the advice of the social worker, we immediately filed a petition for shared custody of the twins. It was only through that litigation, when we were able to obtain the records of the child protective services agency, that Eric finally learned what the sexual abuse allegation was: After returning from a visit with their father, the boys had apparently told their mother that they saw something white and bubbly coming out of Daddy's penis and Daddy said they should make it come out of their penises, too. Rather than talking to Eric about it, the mother called the child abuse hotline.

The minute Eric heard this he knew exactly what the boys were describing. He had taken them to a concert where a member of his band was playing. During the show, the boys had to go to the bathroom. He took them to the men's room and brought both of them with him into one of the bathroom stalls. Eric did not want them to sit on the toilet because it was dirty, so he decided this was a good time to get them to try to pee standing up. Eric peed in the toilet to show them what to do, and they thought it was funny how the pee made white bubbles when it hit the water. They laughed and wanted him to do it again, and he said they should pee in the toilet and they could make white bubbles, too.

Eric was both relieved that he could explain and angry that this was the reason he had not seen his children for close to a year. As injustices go, this was a pretty easy one to undo: All it took was the filing of a petition. A custody hearing was scheduled, the mother hired a lawyer, we got the records of the investigation, we had Eric submit to a psychiatric evaluation, which came up clean and supported the credibility of his story, and then we negotiated a settlement with the mother. Eric got his shared-custody schedule. We never had to go to court.

This case made it through my wall, too. The thought of this poor guy not seeing his kids for ten months because he mistakenly thought he could end up in jail if he tried was just so upsetting. But I never had that pit-of-the-stomach feeling, because it was pretty clear to me right from the beginning that this was essentially a big mistake and as soon as an advocate became involved it would be straightened out. To my mind, it was always a question of when, not if.

SO HERE'S THE THING: When I worked with all these clients, I thought about them in terms of my own life. Darlene, the most. With Susan and Eric, I didn't feel drawn in nearly as much, but I still thought about how it would feel not to have seen my children for most of a year; I thought about what it would be like for a court to keep me in a city where I did not want to be and prevent me from living with the man I loved and with whom I was about to have a baby.

These are exactly the reasons, I think, that many lawyers don't like family law. They don't *want* to relate their clients' circumstances to their own. They want to keep them separated. And they don't want to think about the other side, either; they don't want to experience the painful reality that a win for Susan could forever alter her ex-husband's relationship with his children. A dispute between two corporations, say, could be intellectually interesting (sometimes) but it probably doesn't lead to anxiety dreams about your client giving birth or affect the way you watch your own child sleeping in her bed at night. Those lawyers want more than a wall; they want to live on a different street. I prefer to remain adjacent neighbors, where I can share in the celebrations and the sadness but, at the end of the day, return to my own home and close the door.

The Prenup and the Porsche

On a recent Father's Day, my twenty-four- and twenty-one-year-old daughters and their boyfriends were visiting for the weekend. The day in question was an extremely hot, sticky, late-June-in-Philadelphia Sunday, and in keeping with the occasion, the choice of activity was entirely my husband's. "I want to go to the race car museum," he announced, as we sat around the living room sweating and drinking coffee. Despite having lived in Philly for twenty-two years, I had absolutely no idea what museum he was talking about, and my daughters, though considerably past the eye-rolling stage, made it crystal clear that they thought the morning could be way better spent lounging in an air-conditioned restaurant, eating spinach omelets and toasting their father with mimosas. Josh and Mario, however, whether out of polite deference or genuine interest or probably a combination of both, expressed their enthusiasm for the plan, and it was, after all, Father's Day.

So off the six of us went, in pursuit of exotic automotive delights.

We ended up in a gritty, industrial neighborhood down by the airport, at a huge warehouse you would never find if you weren't looking really hard for it. When I think of a museum, this is not what comes to mind. The place was cavernous. There were no glass cases with artifacts inside, no framed canvases on the walls to ponder. Instead, spread out over acres of cool, dark, cement floors, organized by time and by race track, were what the museum's website describes as "over 60 of the rarest and most significant racing sports cars ever built." The entire collection was donated by one man, who had accumulated these amazing cars over the past fifty years.

As it turned out, we all loved the place. The cars were phenomenal. The girls even forgot about the mimosas. We strolled through a replica of the Mille Miglia in the hills of Italy, gawking at a 1933 Alfa Romeo Monza; went around the corner into Germany, ogling a 1955 Mercedes-Benz with doors that swung upward like a bird's wings (the Gullwing!); then proceeded to Le Mans . . . Who can resist the beauty of a 1956 Maserati 300S? The elegance of design, the marvel of engineering, the embodiment of speed and fantasy and adventure contained in each race car—it was a little boy's fantasy writ large. Men (and there were lots of them there, it being Father's Day) were swooning.

I found myself wondering about the donor. How could one person have amassed so many valuable cars? He must have been determined to build something no one else had; he was clearly a man with a vision. He also must be off-the-charts wealthy to have bought and restored more than sixty of these cars. Each one was worth a small fortune. And he was certainly a guy's guy — is there anything more redolent of testosterone than race cars? So interesting, I mused, what people do with their money, what they hold dear, what they collect and what they display.

JORANI PANG MADE an appointment to see me because her fiancé told her she had to. Jorani explained to me on the phone, in accented English, that her fiancé's lawyer had written a prenuptial agreement that she was supposed to sign before their wedding. Apparently, the lawyer had told him that Jorani needed to have her own lawyer review it before she signed it, and he had given her fiancé my name.

Jorani came to the United States from Cambodia when she was a teenager. She got pregnant in high school, dropped out, and worked at a series of restaurant and bartending jobs while raising her daughter. Somewhere along the way, she met the man she was now engaged to and her world changed radically. When I met her, she was twenty-five, petite, and stunningly beautiful, with long, dark hair, a couture dress, and an enormous diamond engagement ring. Her fiancé was a successful venture capitalist in his late forties. They had been living together for a couple of years, and he was fully supporting her and her eight-year-old daughter. He was financially very generous: She didn't have to work, she had her own credit card for which he paid the bill, no questions asked, and she was encouraged to care for her child, buy beautiful clothing, decorate their home, and generally make his life pleasant. Now he had asked her to marry him.

This may sound like an immigration fairy tale, but there were, as there always are, strings attached. The fiancé did not want to have any financial obligation to Jorani if the relationship ended. So as a condition of marrying her, he asked her to sign a prenuptial agreement waiving all claims she would have had by virtue of being married: She was to waive her interest in any assets that he might acquire during the marriage (investments, retirement funds, real estate), in any increase in the value of the substantial assets he already had (about $12 million worth), and in any alimony. So as not to literally leave her and her daughter out on the street, the prenuptial agreement she brought me to review contained a provision that she was to receive a lump sum of $15,000 for each year they had been married, up to a cap of $150,000, and her personal property. In other words, if they divorced after twenty years of marriage, she would get $150,000 and the designer clothes in her closet.

PRENUPTIAL AGREEMENTS ARE contracts people sign before they get married that govern what will happen if they divorce or if one spouse dies. If you marry without a prenuptial agreement, as the vast majority of people do, and you later divorce, the laws of the state in which you are divorcing will dictate the outcome. As a general rule, those laws will provide for the distribution between spouses of the property acquired during the marriage—houses, cars, bank accounts, investments, pensions—regardless of how the property is titled. Those laws may also provide, as they do in Pennsylvania under certain circumstances, for the payment of alimony from the higher-earning spouse to the lower-earning one for a specified period based on various factors such as the length of the marriage, the age of the parties, and how much money each earns or could earn.

Similarly, if one spouse dies and there is no prenuptial agreement, the laws of the state where the couple resided will determine what happens to the estate of the deceased spouse. Estate laws typically prevent people from entirely disinheriting their husbands or wives. If you are married and write a will leaving all your assets to beneficiaries other than your spouse, your surviving spouse has the right to "elect" against the will and receive a portion of your estate, despite your intent that he or she get nothing at all.

These laws are based on long-accepted policies about marriage, and are primarily designed to protect women and children. Of course, they are now written and applied in a gender-neutral fashion, so that the economically dependent spouse who benefits by getting a share of the other spouse's pension and receiving alimony payments may now be, and not infrequently is, the husband. But the underlying premises remain the same: that marriage is a socially important institution; that contributions to a marriage may be nonmonetary in nature but still have real value; and that when the marriage ends by death or divorce, each spouse should have part of what was acquired together, regardless of who was the breadwinner.

Despite the social consensus about these policies, our legal system is grounded in an even stronger belief in the right of self-determination. You can opt out of all this if you want. You are free to write your own script. However, there are instances where the law imposes limits on what you can contract for. There are laws designed to protect the rights of certain classes of people who have little or no bargaining power. Landlord-tenant laws require landlords to provide certain basic services even if a tenant signs a contract waiving her right to those services. Consumer protection laws require products to meet certain safety standards even if the buyer of the product signs a waiver. Truth-in-lending laws mandate a grace period after certain loan documents are signed, in case the borrower changes his mind. These laws arise out of a public acknowledgment that not all playing fields are level, that the little guy needs protection from contract terms that might be imposed by the powerful guy—the landlord, the manufacturer, or the bank.

So which kind of contract is a prenuptial agreement? Do people engaged to be married stand on equal footing and therefore should whatever they agree to be enforced by the courts? Or is the fiancé who is being asked to waive her (or his) rights in such a vulnerable position that the courts should protect her from the excessive harshness of the result?

IN PENNSYLVANIA, OUR Supreme Court has come down squarely in the equal-footing camp, in a case called *Simeone v. Simeone.* In 1975, a twenty-three-year-old unemployed nurse was engaged to a thirty-nine-year-old neurosurgeon. The night before the wedding, Dr. Simeone presented his almost-wife with a prenuptial agreement prepared by his lawyer and told her to sign it, which she did, without benefit of counsel and without his pointing out to her the legal rights she was surrendering. The terms of the agreement limited Mrs. Simeone to payments of $200 per week from her husband in the event of separation or divorce, up to a maximum of $25,000. The agreement did contain a disclosure as to what assets Dr. Simeone owned at the time, which included a classic-car collection. When the Simeones divorced some ten years later, Dr. Simeone was a very wealthy man. Mrs. Simeone, not surprisingly, was quite unhappy with her $25,000. She challenged the validity of the agreement she had signed in 1975 on the grounds that prenuptial agreements should be given special treatment by the courts as, by their very nature, they are different from arms-length commercial transactions; she argued that the court should uphold a prenuptial agreement only if it makes a "reasonable provision" for the spouse.

By the time this case wound its way up the chain to the Pennsylvania Supreme Court, it was 1990. The feminist wave of the seventies had translated into legislative action in the eighties. In its often-quoted decision, the court went out of its way to soundly reject the women-need-protection theory. In reviewing earlier court decisions on which Mrs. Simeone was relying, Justice Flaherty, who wrote the majority opinion, found that "Such decisions rested upon a belief that spouses are of unequal status and that women are not knowledgeable enough to understand the nature of contracts that they enter. Society has advanced, however, where women are no longer regarded as the 'weaker' party in marriage, or in society generally. . . . Nor is there any viability in the presumption that women are uninformed, uneducated, and readily subject to unfair advantage in marital agreements. Indeed, women nowadays quite often have substantial education, financial awareness, income, and assets."

And as if that weren't enough, the court went on to reference Pennsylvania's Equal Rights Amendment, enacted in

1971, stating that "Paternalistic presumptions and protections that arose to shelter women from the inferiorities and incapacities which they were perceived as having in earlier times have, appropriately, been discarded."

In other words, Mrs. Simeone was out of luck. But apparently not without a fight. There must have been some heated discussions about the case in chambers between the justices, because the *Simeone* decision was not unanimous. In a wonderfully blunt concurring opinion (meaning that the justice agreed with the outcome of the court's decision—he also would have enforced the prenuptial agreement simply because he did not find its terms to be unfair—but not its reasoning), Justice Papadakos wrote that he could not join in the majority opinion because "I fear my colleague does not live in the real world. If I did not know him better I would think that his statements smack of male chauvinism, an attitude that 'you women asked for it, now live with it.' If you want to know about equality of women, just ask them about comparable wages for comparable work. Just ask them about sexual harassment in the workplace. Just ask them about sexual discrimination in the Executive Suites of big business. And the list of discrimination goes on and on."

Justice Papadakos's clear-eyed observations regarding the actual, rather than the legal, status of women in the United Stated in 1990 notwithstanding, it is the majority opinion in *Simeone* that rules, and two decades later it is still the controlling law regarding prenuptial agreements in Pennsylvania. Practical meaning? They can be produced for signing during the walk down the aisle. They don't have to be fair. They don't have to be even a little bit fair. As long as each party discloses his or her assets—the one requirement to make such an agreement valid—the courts will uphold and enforce the terms of the deal.

WHAT *SIMEONE* MEANS to Jorani Pang is this: If she, who was not a native English speaker, lacked a high school degree, and had no real understanding of the American legal system, had signed the prenuptial agreement her fiancé gave her, she would have been limited to those $15,000 annual payments if they divorced, even if her husband had amassed hundreds of millions of dollars in investments during the time they were married. When I meet with a client in this situation (woman with no wealth, marrying man with lots of it), my job is to advise her about all the rights she's giving up. I feel that I have done well if the client goes back to her fiancé, tells him she's not signing the agreement, he says okay, and the marriage proceeds.

That wouldn't work for Jorani. It turned out that she had no bargaining power, because her fiancé didn't care if they got married. He was perfectly happy with things the way they were. He was agreeing to marry as a concession to her; in exchange, she would have to sign a prenup. Therefore, as annoyed as she became when she realized what she was being asked to give up, as a practical matter Jorani and I knew she was still going to be in a better position married than not married. Fifteen thousand dollars a year is a whole lot better than nothing a year. So, resigned to having to make the deal, my goal became sweetening it.

When you have no real leverage in a negotiation, nothing to withhold in order to gain something else, you have to resort to moral arguments. I figured that Jorani's fiancé probably liked to think of himself as a generous guy. No one wants to be labeled a cheapskate. Plus, he presumably loved Jorani. Didn't he want to be more magnanimous? That was my pitch to his lawyer. Suppose she was a loyal and loving wife who dedicated herself to his happiness and comfort for fifteen years. Supposed he fell in love with someone else, and wanted to move on. Did he really intend for her to be left with no source of support, minimal job skills, and a check that wouldn't even pay for a studio apartment in their swanky Center City neighborhood? Surely that wouldn't be right. And what would his stepdaughter, whom he would be helping to raise, think of that? I called his lawyer and asked him to put this scenario in front of his client. I advised Jorani to make similar appeals at home.

The result, no doubt due more to her powers of persuasion applied directly to her fiancé than to my telephone conversations with opposing counsel, was a slow negotiation that increased the annual payments to something far more reasonable if the marriage lasted for a long time. We settled on $2,500 for each month of marriage to a cap of $500,000, plus a fund for Jorani's daughter to which her fiancé would contribute a set amount every year. This was a lot better than where we started, and a whole lot better than the nothing she would get if they didn't marry, so Jorani and I were satisfied.

BACK TO THE car museum on Father's Day. Something kept nagging at me, a glimmer of recognition, some faint feeling of familiarity. As we were nearing the end of the collection and I was bidding farewell to the gorgeous Maserati and thinking miserably about my dented Honda CRV, a lightbulb went on. We were standing in the Simeone Foundation Museum. The man who owned the race cars was *that* Dr. Simeone. This was the classic-car collection, by now greatly expanded, to which Mrs. Simeone waived all claim back in 1975! No wonder she was hopping mad. My gaze swept over the millions of dollars of metal and rubber and beautiful design I had just seen and I imagined Mrs. Simeone, clutching her $25,000 check, standing at the locked door to the museum, nose pressed to the glass, looking in at the riches she missed out on.

I was so overcome by this image and the realization about where we were that I had to drag the entire family out of the museum and into the sweltering heat of the parking lot to deliver a lecture about the *Simeone* case and the law of prenuptial agreements in Pennsylvania. My husband said he already knew. Josh and Mario were interested but wanted to get back to the cars. My daughters' eyes widened, then narrowed; sympathy for Mrs. Simeone, outrage at the Unfairness of It All, concern that their mother might be talking a little too loudly in the parking lot—I could see the threads of interest and concern swirling in their beautiful blue eyes.

I guess I was all riled up because, well, what about my daughters? Do they still, here in the twenty-first century, need the (admittedly) paternalistic protection of the state? Many would say they do not. But I'm not convinced that the world has changed that much. In fact, from where I sit, I have a pretty good idea that it hasn't. So for my girls, I worry, I educate, and I tell them not to sign any contracts their mother hasn't reviewed. So far, so good.

Stefan

Iused to think I knew a lot about domestic violence. I worked in a battered-women's shelter for a year after college, and that experience propelled me into law school. As a young lawyer, I took a job at a victims' services agency in New York City where I was specifically dealing with domestic violence issues; when I moved to Philadelphia, I worked in the legal center of an organization called Women Against Abuse, representing victims of domestic violence in protection-order and custody cases. When I went into private practice a few years later, many of my cases involved domestic violence. So when Stefan Stromberg, a thirty-year-old artist and waitress, hired me to represent her in obtaining a protection order against her husband and initiating divorce proceedings, it was exactly the type of case I typically handled. I was knowledgeable about the law and comfortable with the issues.

Stefan came to her first appointment with her mother,

Paula. Paula seemed anxious; Stefan was calm. I learned that Stefan's husband, Larry, was a personal trainer who also made grade-B horror films. Larry had raped and assaulted Stefan in the past. She had never been injured so badly that she needed medical treatment, and there had been no recent physical incidents. However, Larry had been stalking her—following her, tracking where she was all the time, making threats, and generally causing her anxiety. She had filed for a protection order to keep him away from her. The hearing was coming up. She had also decided to seek a divorce and was in the process of moving out of their apartment. Paula had traveled from her home in Florida to help find a lawyer for her daughter and to help her pack and move. Paula wanted Stefan to relocate to Florida, far away from Larry. Stefan wanted to find an apartment in Philadelphia, in a high-rise building with security so she wouldn't be looking over her shoulder all the time. There was some tension between mother and daugher about this issue. Paula was clearly very worried and wanted to put as much distance between Stefan and Larry as possible, but Stefan didn't want to leave her life in Philly.

I went over the facts involved in the protection-order case, got the information I needed to file a divorce complaint, and told Stefan I would meet her at court for the hearing, which was scheduled on the following Friday.

The hearing for the protection order turned out not to be

a hearing at all, because the case settled. Larry Stromberg was there without a lawyer, and he agreed right away to the entry of the order against him so there was no need to put on Stefan's testimony about the past abuse and the stalking. We resolved it all in the waiting area outside the courtroom. He understood that Stefan was moving out of their apartment, and we talked briefly about the division of some furniture. He was an attractive man, polite and friendly to me, and I recall shaking his hand after he signed the agreement for the protection order.

I left court that day thinking that the situation was well under control. The past violence had not been severe, nothing had happened recently except the stalking, and now a protection order was in place. The existence of this order meant that the police would have to respond immediately if Larry went near his wife. Stefan was moving over the weekend to a new place, her mother was in town to help her do that, and the following week we would file for divorce. It was 1996. I had been practicing law for eleven years, and Stefan's case was similar to tens, if not hundreds, of domestic violence matters I had handled. I went home from work that Friday and did not think about Stefan over the weekend.

EARLY MONDAY MORNING I got a call at home. Stefan Stromberg and her mother had been murdered the day before, stabbed to death as they were packing up Stefan's belongings at her apartment. Larry Stromberg was the suspect. He had run from the crime scene into Fairmount Park, where he was apparently hiding. There was a citywide manhunt going on for him that morning.

To say I was paralyzed, or devastated, or grief stricken, or anything else, would not come close to conveying my emotions. It was (and I hope will remain) the single lowest moment of my professional life. I felt like an absolute failure. I had done my job, gotten my client a protection order, but I had failed to accomplish what she had looked to me to provide for her: safety. And I felt guilty for not assessing this case correctly. I racked my brain about what I should have done differently. Although I couldn't think of any action not taken or words unspoken, this provided me no solace. It was my internal failure to recognize the danger Stefan was in, my lack of foresight, that took my breath away.

I was also scared. I live near the part of Fairmount Park where Larry Stromberg was at large. My name and address were in the phone book. My daughters, then ages ten and six, attended school in the neighborhood. He had just committed a horrific crime for which he surely knew he would be caught and put away for the rest of his life; he had nothing to lose. Maybe he would come after me or my kids. Or maybe he would show up downtown at my office. Yet those fears were so overshadowed by how sick I felt about Stefan and her poor mother that I pushed them aside. I did what I always did. I took my kids to school and went to work.

A day later, Larry Stromberg turned himself in. I was no longer worried about whether he would come after me or my family, but I was still operating in a daze. A few days afterward, I was surprised by a call from the judge who had signed Stefan's protection order. Even though she'd had little contact with the case, as there had not been an actual hearing, she clearly felt connected to it. The judge wanted to know if I was okay. She told me that she would be happy to arrange counseling through the court for me and members of my staff if we wanted it. I was so touched by the call. Although at an intellectual level I knew I did not cause the murders, it helped me to know that others didn't view it as if I had, that in fact my colleagues were concerned about me. It helped because inside I had this miserable aching feeling that, had I done something differently, Stefan and Paula would still be alive.

LARRY STROMBERG WAS tried and convicted of Stefan's and Paula's murders and sentenced to life in prison without parole. I testified at the trial, which was a grimly satisfying experience. I told the jury what Stefan had hired me to do for her and described our court appearance two days before Larry committed the murders. I took her file with me to court and turned it over to the judge after he ordered me to. His order allowed me to break the attorney-client privilege that otherwise would have still existed between me and my dead client.

Sometime later I was asked to participate in a fatality review conducted by a coalition of representatives from the district attorney's office, the police department, battered women's advocacy groups, and other agencies whose work involved the prevention of domestic violence. The goal was to analyze domestic violence homicide cases to see what, if anything, could have prevented the death, what systems could be strengthened or tweaked or put in place. I remember sitting at the head of a long table in a musty conference room in some government agency as the autopsy photographs were passed around. My friend at the D.A.'s office who had asked me to participate made sure to tell me what was being circulated, and told me I did not have to view the photographs if they would be too disturbing. I actually did want to look. I felt I owed it to my client and her mother to see what happened to them, to look, for the first time, at the injuries inflicted on them. The photos were stark and upsetting. They made me cry. But everyone on the committee was understanding and allowed me a few moments to get it together before I told them what I knew about the events leading up to the murders. I left feeling shaken by the photographs but comforted by the collective brain power and knowledge and commitment in the room.

It was hard to know how to help Stefan's surviving family, but we figured out a plan. At the request of Stefan's stepfather (Paula's husband), I filed what's called a wrongful death action on behalf of Stefan and Paula's estates. First

I had to get the stepfather appointed as administrator of both women's estates so he could bring the action on their behalf. Since Stefan was married at the time of her death, Larry was actually her next of kin. Fortunately, there's a statute in Pennsylvania that prohibits a person who kills a spouse from serving as administrator of the spouse's estate. The purpose of the wrongful death action was to obtain a large judgment against Larry Stromberg so that, even though he was serving a life sentence without parole, in the highly unlikely event that he made any money while he was in prison for the filmmaking work he had done before the murders, he would not see any profit from it; any money he might be entitled to would have to go toward satisfying the judgment.

In a wrongful death suit in which the defendant has been criminally convicted, liability is not an issue; the identity of the murderer is conclusively established. The court need only determine the extent of the pain and suffering experienced by the plaintiffs before they died. Given the gruesome nature of this crime, it seems that it was probably a lot. Mother and daughter both had defensive wounds on their hands consistent with trying to fight Larry off. Paula was a small, thin woman, but I imagined that her mother's rage must have risen up within her as she tried to protect her daughter. At the assessment of damages hearing, I presented evidence about the murders to the judge and asked for a judgment of $1,000,000 against Larry Stromberg. He entered an order in that amount. That million-dollar judgment sits there, to this day, unsatisfied.

Writing about this experience is so different from writing about other cases and clients, in which I change names and identifying information to protect privacy, in which the clients I am writing about live and breathe. Everything I have written here about Stefan is a matter of public record. Her name and her story were told in the press, in the testimony I was ordered to give in the criminal case in which Larry Stromberg was convicted, and in the civil case in which we were awarded the monetary judgment against him. There are no secrets to keep, because two lives ended and the story I am telling is now history, not part of the fabric of an ongoing existence.

It sounds trite to say that this experience taught me a lesson, but it absolutely did. It taught me something essential about domestic violence and my role as an advocate. I do not know what is going to happen. I cannot predict, I cannot grade or assess, I cannot sort out the high risk from the low risk. I am completely humbled in that department. As a result, I now think about every domestic violence case as a potential homicide. If my client tells me she is scared for her life, even though I cannot see any history of events that would indicate why she might be, I honor that fear.

I don't think I operate in a practical way any differently

than I used to. It's more of a shift of mindset. I knew, when I represented Stefan and all the women before her, that the client's assessment of risk was key. I always knew to say, You're the one who knows him best; I knew to act on her wishes, to advocate for her position. But with Stefan, I believed I knew something about the level of danger she was in. Now I know I don't. Now I know I can shake a smiling man's hand in court one day and two days later he can stab my client to death. Now, if opposing counsel tries to minimize the violence in a case or imply that my client is overreacting, I cut him right off. I tell him: I had a client who was murdered. Neither of us knows what your client is capable of. You and I need to assume the worst because the worst sometimes comes to pass. I find that this speech is very effective and I have had to make it a number of times. This is Stefan's legacy to me. Human beings are fundamentally unpredictable, nobody is safe, and two beautiful women can lose their lives in a storm of violence in a matter of minutes. The unimaginable can and does happen.

ANATOMY OF A TRIAL, PART I:
The Case

Jimmy just turned five. His mother tells me he's a kid who can't sit still; he's always running, jumping, fidgeting, playing. His big sister, Kaitlyn, is eight; she's quiet, a reader and a thinker. I represent their mom, Beth Foster, in her divorce from their dad. The kids live with Beth in a small ranchhouse located in a modest, working-class suburb of Philadelphia. Their dad used to live there, too, but he moved into an apartment about four months ago, after we filed the divorce complaint. Every other weekend, Kaitlyn and Jimmy go to his place on Fridays after school and Brian brings them back to Beth on Sunday evenings, and every Wednesday night they stay over with him as well. Brian categorically refuses to communicate with Beth, so she has no idea about what goes on during these visits, except what the kids tell her.

The situation is tense. According to Beth, Brian is both emotionally and physically abusive. Not very often, but the unpredictability of it meant that she was always on edge.

Sometimes he would come home from work in a bad mood and start cursing at her, throwing plates and pans around the kitchen; once he punched a hole in their bedroom door. When he was in this state, Beth might manage to keep herself and the kids out of his way all evening, only to be woken up repeatedly during the night and screamed at for not caring enough about him, for not doing this or that, for, essentially, failing to make him feel better. And on a few occasions, it escalated to the point where he would slap her or pinch her, hard. When Beth decided she couldn't take it anymore, she hired me. I helped her file for divorce, and Brian reluctantly agreed to move out. In the divorce complaint, we included a request for primary custody of the children. The court required us to go to a custody "conciliation," which we did, but we weren't able to reach a settlement, so the case was scheduled for trial.

The every-other-weekend-and-Wednesday-night custody order is temporary, a compromise worked out between me and Brian's lawyer to carry us through until the trial. Neither Beth nor Brian likes it. Beth doesn't want the kids there overnight during the week. She says Brian feeds them junk, doesn't help Kaitlyn with her homework, lets them stay up as late as they want, and doesn't take them to school (preschool, in Jimmy's case) on time the next morning. She thinks it's disruptive and stressful for them, that they should have the same routine every school night. She's lukewarm about the alternate weekends, too, although she is aware from her discussions with me that there's probably little we can do about that, as it's a pretty minimal custody schedule as far as the court is concerned.

While these issues are important to Beth, they're not her core concerns. What's keeping her up at night is the fear that if she isn't around, the kids will become the target of Brian's unpredictable, bullying behavior.

She had started to see glimpses of that before he left, especially toward Jimmy, who tends to be defiant and also to break things, which sets Brian off. The only specific example she was able to describe to me was when Jimmy refused to eat some chicken she had cooked for dinner and Brian took off his belt and tied Jimmy to his chair at the dining room table. Jimmy started to cry and thrash around, and despite Beth's pleading, his dad just tied him tighter and made him stay there while Brian essentially force-fed him the chicken, which Jimmy couldn't even swallow because he was choking and crying so hard. These types of power struggles were very disturbing to Beth, and she feels that without her mediating influence they will be much worse when Brian is alone with the kids.

Brian, not surprisingly, has the opposite view. Through conversations with his lawyer and Brian's presentation at the conciliation, I know that he wants everything to be "fifty-fifty" in their divorce, meaning the property should be divided that way and so should the kids. He's looking to have Kaitlyn and Jimmy alternate homes on a weekly basis.

He says that Beth's concern about school-night routine is just a sign of her obsessive, rigid, and controlling nature; they simply have different parenting styles. He's more laid back and more playful, he takes the kids camping and fishing, and he's looking forward to being a Cub Scout leader when Jimmy is old enough to join a troop next year.

Brian admits that he was late getting the kids to school the first couple of Thursdays, because he wasn't used to handling the morning routine and didn't leave enough time; now he's got it down and they've been on time. He says Kaitlyn hasn't needed help with her homework and this is an area where he and Beth just have a different approach: He believes that Kaitlyn is old enough to take responsibility for her schoolwork and Beth shouldn't hover over her or correct her mistakes. If she doesn't finish it, or she does it wrong and gets a bad grade as a result, that is a life lesson his daughter needs to learn. And, yes, they have pizza for dinner on Wednesday nights, which the kids love; yes, he lets them stay up later than Beth does because they have so little time with him and because they're not ready to go to sleep at 8 p.m. and because, frankly, he's their father and it's not up to Beth to tell him what time he has to put his children to bed.

I have also communicated to Brian's lawyer the more serious concerns; I told him about Brian's rampages, about the fact that the kids may have witnessed some of them (including their father breaking Beth's favorite plates, which she inherited from her grandmother) and about the incident where he tied Jimmy to the chair with his belt. Brian says Beth is exaggerating and distorting; that she's the one who has historically initiated fights with him because he isn't doing something just the way she wants him to; that there was a plate-smashing incident but it was Beth who broke the first one; and Jimmy, who is small for his age, until recently still sat in a booster seat at the dining room table, and Brian used his belt in place of the broken strap on the seat, just to make sure Jimmy didn't fall out.

Our trial date is in three weeks, and Beth and I are in the process of figuring out what witnesses to call and what documents to introduce.

Then everything changes. On a Friday morning in February a very upset Beth calls me at the office. The previous evening when she undressed Jimmy to give him his bath, she noticed that he had a massive, purple bruise encircling his upper right arm. He did not have it on Wednesday when she dropped him off at school, and he had spent Wednesday night at his father's. She asked Jimmy how he got it. He said he didn't know. She called Brian, who didn't answer her calls until she texted him that it was an emergency involving Jimmy, and asked him how Jimmy got the bruise. He told her he didn't know. He said that he noticed it Thursday morning when he was helping Jimmy get dressed, that Jimmy didn't know where the bruise came from and that he figured maybe Jimmy fell at school on Wednesday or

Kaitlyn did it, or whatever. But it was just a bruise and it didn't seem to be bothering Jimmy, so he didn't think it was a big deal.

When Beth dropped Jimmy off at preschool earlier that morning, she showed his arm to Marla Peres, the preschool teacher, and asked her if Jimmy had been involved in any accidents or fights during the past two days. Marla said no, and asked Beth if she had any idea what might have caused the bruise. Beth told her that Jimmy wasn't saying, but he had been in his father's care when it appeared. She confided in Marla that she and Brian were separated and that Brian had been abusive to her and to Jimmy in the past. Brian must have done this, she told Marla, and then warned Jimmy not to tell anyone because they were in the middle of a custody battle.

Marla responded by describing an interaction she saw between Brian and Jimmy when Brian dropped him off at school one morning. It struck her as strange. Jimmy, who usually ran into the classroom to see his friends, was out in the hallway, crying, and didn't want to come into the room. She saw Brian bent over him, talking in a loud, harsh whisper. She couldn't hear what he was saying, but whatever it was, Jimmy started to cry harder. Brian then brought Jimmy through the doorway into the classroom, turned around, and left without hanging up Jimmy's jacket or putting Jimmy's lunch box in his cubby or even saying good-bye. Jimmy was still tearful and it took him a little while to return to his normal boisterous self. Beth said she wasn't surprised, because Brian was really hard on Jimmy and it was worse since they separated.

Marla looked at the bruise on Jimmy's arm again and told Beth that she was mandated to report suspected child abuse; based on what Beth was telling her, she was going to have to call in a report to the state child abuse hotline.

I ask Beth to photograph the bruise and email me the photos, which she does. The bruise is big and purple and runs from Jimmy's elbow almost to his shoulder, but I can't make out any finger- or handprints. Jimmy is supposed to go to his father's this afternoon for the weekend. Beth does not want him to. I tell her that as long as the current court order is in effect, she has to comply with it or risk being held in contempt of court, which can mean fines or having to pay Brian's attorney's fees or, most significantly, losing credibility with the judge who might ultimately be hearing her custody case. Beth is unpersuaded. How, she asks me, can I expect her to deliver her little boy into the arms of a man who has seriously injured him, lied about it, and told Jimmy to lie about it? I repeat my speech about how I can't advise her to violate a court order, but I know if it were me, and I thought my kids were really in danger — which, in this case, I'm on the fence about, but I'm not Beth — I would say to hell with the order.

Beth decides to keep both kids with her and emails Brian at 5 p.m. that because of the bruise and the child abuse investigation, which will shortly ensue, she is not going to take the kids over to his house. I tell her she can't do that, and she responds that she is going to anyway. Despite the emphatic advice I am bound to give, I'm not too worried, because the social worker from Child Protective Services already contacted her, an investigation is in fact under way, and I don't think the judge will be too upset about Beth's withholding the kids, or at least Jimmy, in this context.

On Monday, Beth calls the office to tell me that Ms. Williams, the caseworker from CPS, is coming to her house that evening to interview her and Jimmy. And maybe Kaitlyn. I advise her to clean the house, be polite, and tell the worker about Brian's history of abuse against her and about the incident in which Brian tied Jimmy to the chair and force-fed him. The next day Beth calls again; she's very distressed. Apparently Jimmy said the same thing to the social worker that he had said to her, that he doesn't remember how he got the bruise, and Kaitlyn had nothing to say about it, either. Despite the now rapidly fading bruise, the social worker did recommend that Beth take Jimmy to the emergency room at a nearby hospital where they have a child abuse protocol and they'll do a forensic exam. She also told Beth that unless the doctor can link the bruise to an adult's intentional act rather than a typical five-year-old's scrape-up, she will have to "unfound" the investigation. She won't tell Beth if she has already interviewed Brian, but Beth knows how that went (or is about to go). Brian can be charming and

he certainly would have told the social worker, with a rueful smile, that he and Beth are right in the middle of a very
nasty custody case, that Beth is high strung and overpro-
tective, and that she runs to the pediatrician's office about
every little bump and scrape.

Beth takes Jimmy to the emergency room and, after waiting for almost three hours, is finally seen by a pediatric ER
doc. He takes a medical history, talks directly to Jimmy
about the cause of the bruise ("I don't know"), examines
Jimmy thoroughly, looks especially carefully at the yellow-
ing bruise, and makes notes in the special chart used for
the child abuse exam, marking an "x" on the upper right
arm of a drawing of a figure that looks uncomfortably like
the chalk outline of a body drawn on the ground by police after a homicide. He tells Beth there's no way to know
what caused the bruise. While a bruise encircling the upper
arm is not typical of a play-related accident, which would
more commonly cause bruises to bony protrusions like el-
bows and knees, he can't see any imprint of a hand or a
finger or an object such as a belt buckle. There is no medical
link—and no link from the interview—to lead to the conclusion that the bruise was caused intentionally by anyone,
much less a parent.

BRIAN'S LAWYER, AN older, bald, perpetually tanned
guy named Francis DiLorenzo, who's big in suburban Republican politics, is getting hot under the collar. Brian's now

missed a whole weekend with the kids and it looks like Beth's not going to let him have them on Wednesday, either. Francis calls me, tells me my client's making a mistake. He's going to file a petition asking that she be immediately held in contempt. He might even file a counterclaim for primary custody because she's clearly alienating the children from their father, and they need to be removed from her hostile and controlling grip. "Do what you have to," I tell him, trying to sound nonchalant; "My client is not going to turn the kids over while the investigation is going on, and you know Judge Diamond wouldn't expect her to."

This is only partly accurate. CPS has no legal authority at this point to prevent the children from spending time with their father. But Judge Diamond might agree with me that it's the better practice to wait, "to err on the side of the children's safety," as judges love to say, until the investigation is complete. Then again, he might not agree and be pissed off at my client and maybe at me, too. I'm an officer of the court; I can't advise a client to violate a court order (which I didn't do, but I didn't push very hard against doing it, either). Yet I have no choice but to defend the validity of Beth's actions because she is adamant about refusing to let the children go to Brian's.

Two days later, Beth receives a letter in the mail from Child Protective Services. The report of suspected child abuse is unfounded and the case has been closed. Although she anticipated this, Beth is distraught nonetheless. She wants to know what I can do to protect her children. What action can we take? She does not want them to go back to their father's house until he gets some professional help. With Jimmy not saying how he got the bruise and the report coming back unfounded, we don't have enough to seek an immediate, emergency order from the court suspending Brian's visitation, and I tell her so. The trial is in two weeks, I remind her. That's our opportunity to present whatever evidence we can about this issue—the fact that it happened during Brian's custodial time, and that Brian was abusive to Beth and Jimmy in the past—so that the judge can take it into account when making his decision about the custody schedule.

The following week, Beth is giving Jimmy a bath and Jimmy is playing with his yellow rubber tugboat. All of a sudden, he looks up at her and says: "Daddy is mean."

"Why do you say that?" Beth asks. "Did he do something to you?"

"He hurt me."

"How did he hurt you? Did he hurt your arm? Is that how you got the bruise?"

Jimmy nods. "Daddy hurt my arm."

"How?"

"He said I was bad and he squeezed my arm really hard."

"Why did he do that?"

"I spilled grape juice on the rug and I was supposed to clean it up and I didn't do it right. He grabbed my arm really hard and made me wipe it."

"Jimmy, why didn't you tell me this when I asked you about the bruise?"

"Because Daddy told me not to tell you. He said it was my fault because I spilled the juice but if I told you you'd be mad at him. And then I couldn't come to his house and he would just have Kaitlyn come for the weekend." Jimmy started to cry.

This is what Beth tells me. I wasn't there and I have no way of knowing if Jimmy was accurately describing what happened with his father, if he told his mother all this because at some level he knew it was what she wanted to hear, or if he said something much less specific that Beth has spun into a definitive indictment of Brian's conduct. All are possible. But I have to take my marching orders from Beth, and she's convinced that this is exactly what went down. She wants Brian's visitation suspended and she doesn't want to wait until the trial. She says this is how it started with her; a threat here, a slap there. And then it escalated. She doesn't want the same for her kids. And now that Jimmy has revealed the truth, Beth is convinced that we have the ammunition we need.

I'm not so sure. With the trial date now less than two weeks away, I am positive we would not be granted an earlier date for a separate hearing on this specific issue. However, I do think Jimmy's revelation has the potential to make our case much stronger at trial, and we might even be able to convince the judge to suspend Brian's visits while he gets some kind of treatment. I'm thinking a course of anger management therapy and parenting classes. In order to pull that off, we will need Judge Diamond to hear what Jimmy said and to believe it. Either Jimmy will have to tell him directly or he will have to let Beth testify about Jimmy's bathtub confession.

I know that Francis is going to have a field day with this. He's going to argue that Beth is out to nail Brian because he had an affair and left her (he did, and she says she could care less); that this whole incident is just a minor accident that she has totally blown out of proportion in an attempt to gain leverage going into the custody trial; and if Jimmy did report something like this to Beth, it's only the result of Beth's coaching him repeatedly until she finally got what she was looking for, all in service of punishing Brian for his transgressions. That will be his theme: a woman scorned. Nonetheless, if Beth is right and Brian is out of control to the extent that days before a custody trial, when his parenting is clearly under the microscope, he would squeeze his five-year-old son's arm to the point of creating a huge bruise, it is very serious. What will it be next?

I call Beth, who has difficulty understanding that the courts are not immediately accessible to her to address this crisis, but she reluctantly accepts my decision against filing the emergency petition. Let's focus on the trial, I tell her, and we set up appointments for her to come to my office to prepare her testimony. I know I'm going to have to break it to her that Judge Diamond may not permit her to testify to what Jimmy told her during his bath, but I'd rather do so in person. I'm not looking forward to that conversation, in which I will need to explain the rationale behind the rule against hearsay, and she will tell me it's wrong and unfair. I've had that talk before, with other clients in other cases, and it never goes well.

Money Culture

Talking about money is our last taboo. It's surprising, given the complete disintegration of privacy about some of the most intimate aspects of people's lives. Even in post–*Jerry Springer,* –*Jersey Shore* America, we continue to accept the curiously old-fashioned social convention that financial information is not for sharing. I doubt that most of us could say how much our closest friends earn, how much they have saved, or what balances, if any, they carry on their credit cards. And we wouldn't presume to ask. In my job, though, I ask, and people tell me. In fact, they can hardly wait to tell me. Within ten minutes of meeting with a new client I usually know how much she and her husband earn, and by the end of the consultation I know what they spend and save, whether they pool their money or keep it separate, how much debt they have, and whether these subjects are related to the reason they are divorcing.

Which they often are. Clashes about spending, saving, and borrowing are a common complaint. Also, sometimes there's a total disconnect between perception and reality. Like the man who makes $250,000 a year but complains to me that he's had the same coat for a decade because he has no money to buy new clothes. Or my elegant heiress who is aghast at the prospect that she might ever have to spend any principal, because in her family of origin, the expectation was that one should be able to live entirely off the income from one's stock portfolio, thus preserving it for the next generation. Or my Catholic school–secretary client who racked up close to a hundred thousand dollars of credit card debt on furniture, clothing, and vacations over the course of a ten-year marriage, with no idea how the bills would ever be paid.

I find all this money talk extremely interesting. I'm particularly partial to the how-much-do-people-make topic. Want to earn the most money possible without a college degree? Sales, hands down. I represented a man whose wife worked part time from home, selling telecommunications systems; she made over $400,000 per year. Teach art at a small, prestigious private elementary school and you might make so little that you qualify for food stamps. Teach art at a large suburban public high school and you could make close to six figures. Think doctors make the big bucks? Not necessarily; there's an enormous spread. A pediatrician at a teaching hospital might earn just barely more than the public school art teacher, while her radiation oncologist spouse who also owns an interest in a surgical center is pulling in a cool million. And academics? A big variation there, as well. The archaeologist who is employable only within academia comes cheap, whereas his colleague teaching computer science across the street at the business school is likely to be earning three or four times more. (But still not as much as my client's wife who sold phone systems!)

And then there are lawyers. I have many lawyer clients, and most earn more than I do. Sometimes lots more. Often by a factor of five. And many are younger and have been practicing for less time. It's very irritating. Family law is not a lucrative side of the profession, that's for sure.

Another thing I've learned is that every marriage has its own money culture. Some people keep all their funds separate, put their paychecks into personal checking and savings accounts, and divvy up the household bills. They will say, "He pays the mortgage and I pay the gas, electric, and cable." Or, "When we go out to dinner, we split the check." This is one instance where my personal feelings are completely at odds with my professional role. From the divorce lawyer perspective, there's nothing wrong with separate accounts, and there's potentially a significant advantage, because funds that are gifted or inherited are likely to be kept in those separate accounts, and then, under Pennsylvania law, they don't have to be shared with the other spouse in a divorce. But, personally, I find this version of marriage unappealing. It seems distasteful to me to treat my husband like a roommate I found on craigslist. For me, marriage is about putting yourselves in one financial boat, about rising and falling together.

That may be what I feel, but it's not what I would ever tell a client. I am acutely aware that this admittedly rather sentimental viewpoint represents nothing more than the money culture that has evolved in my own marriage. It carries no professional weight whatsoever.

And, anyway, joint accounts do not guarantee shared knowledge. Despite having two names on the checks, some of my clients are totally in the dark about important financial matters, such as how much money their spouses make. I always scratch my head about this—I just can't quite understand how it plays out. Try to imagine the dinner table conversation: "Honey, how was your day?" "Great! My boss told me I'm getting a bonus next week." "Fantastic! How much is it?" "Umm, I'd rather not say." Really? But this is not uncommon. One client told me that she had no idea how much her husband earned, and when I asked gently if they filed joint tax returns, she told me yes, but when he handed her the returns to sign, he would cover up the page so she couldn't see anything but the signature lines. When she asked why he did this, he said it was because they were operating on a "need to know" basis. Apparently, he never felt that she needed to know, and she hadn't thought so either, until she was sitting in my office feeling embarrassed that she lacked this basic information.

It can be much worse. I represented a woman whose

husband hit her when he was angry and belittled her the rest of the time. He was a comptroller at a large corporation and he carried his profession into their home in a particularly sick and evil way. My client had no independent access to money; her husband would dole it out as he saw fit. The system was that if she needed money for household expenses, say, groceries, he made her submit a requisition stating what she intended to purchase and how much she estimated it would cost. He would review the requisition and mark it "approved" or "denied" and, if approved, give her the money. She had to provide him with the receipt after she made the purchases, so he could verify that it lined up with the requisition. If it didn't, she would be punished. This would have been hard to believe had I not seen with my own eyes the little slips of paper listing, in her careful handwriting, what she intended to buy at the drugstore, with the red "approved" written across it in a bigger, bolder hand.

At the other end of the one-spouse-controls-the-money spectrum, there are those happy-go-lucky types who are blissfully ignorant of their family finances not because the other spouse is keeping the information secret, but simply because the family division of labor has evolved such that one person handles all the money and the other completely trusts him or her to do so. It's a chore that one spouse often ends up taking sole charge of, kind of like groceries or laundry. This works fine until that trust thing unravels. Then the blissful ignorance can turn into feelings of foolishness and vulnerability because, let's face it, managing the brokerage account is not really equivalent to making sure the socks get clean. When a client I'm meeting with for the first time cannot answer my most basic questions ("How much do you owe on your mortgage?" "What's in your savings and investment accounts?" "Does your husband have any retirement benefits?"), I wonder how she can operate in the world, not having an understanding of the financial landscape that surrounds and supports her. It would make me so anxious.

Then I think about Alan and I totally understand. My husband, were he sitting in a chair in a divorce lawyer's office (God forbid), couldn't answer any of those questions even close to accurately. And that doesn't make him anxious; it makes him happy. Long ago, after a stint in which I insisted he pay all the bills so he'd understand our finances better—causing me to become increasingly stressed by constantly worrying that he hadn't paid the mortgage on time and causing him to become increasingly irritated that I was breathing down his neck—we both realized this was a ridiculous way to divide household responsibilities. He likes making money (who doesn't?), but he hates dealing with it. He is both overwhelmed by and uninterested in bills, investments, and taxes. He is an architect, an artist, and a musician; he is a thoroughly right-brain kind of guy.

I, on the other hand, have a highly functional left brain.

I wouldn't say I love managing money, but I derive great satisfaction from setting up systems for paying bills, talking to our financial adviser about investments, figuring out when to refinance our mortgage, strategizing about the best way to pay our kids' college tuitions. On Alan's personal unpleasantness scale, these activities are right up there with having a root canal. And, like my client, he never looks at our tax returns before he signs them. I hand them to him, I tell him where to sign, he does it and gives me back the pen.

But unlike my client with the domineering husband, Alan and I are not operating on a "need to know" basis, because I so wish he wanted to know. I would be more than happy to review the returns in detail and explain what my K-1 means, what stock we sold, and why we're paying capital gains tax. Then he could really appreciate all the time and skill and care I put into handling all this! But no such luck, because he and I both know he'd be asleep before I got through the second page of the 1040. So we muddle on this way, and it works for us. So long as we stay married, that is; I am acutely aware that it would not stand him in good stead if we split up. Hopefully, that's not going to happen. After all, he does all the grocery shopping.

GENDER CERTAINLY FACTORS into attitudes toward money, as well. I'm thinking about Bob Morse, a calm, friendly, forty-three year old who's a founder and part owner of an energy consulting firm. He's divorcing his wife of fifteen years. Bob's annual income varies depending on how well his business is doing in any given year, but lately it's been hovering in the $150,000–$200,000 range. He is the breadwinner in the family. His wife, although trained as a nurse, has not worked outside the home for twelve years. Her certifications have lapsed and her skills are rusty; she will need retraining in order to return to the health-care market. Their children are twelve and seven. Bob and his wife were working-class kids who made good, and just about everything they acquired during their marriage — equity in a five-bedroom house on the Main Line, a small place at the Jersey shore two blocks from the beach, Bob's interest in his company and his retirement savings — is a direct result of Bob working fourteen-hour days, six days a week, fifty weeks a year. He earned it all, and his wife took on all the household and child-care responsibilities so that he could.

Bob and I are meeting to review a settlement proposal sent to us by his wife's attorney. The proposal is to give 60 percent of their assets to her and 40 percent to him, which would result in her keeping the house on the Main Line, receiving 60 percent of Bob's retirement account, and getting $100,000 in cash from Bob to buy out her share of his company. That's cash Bob doesn't have, so he would have to borrow it. He would keep the shore house, the remaining 40 percent of his retirement account, and the company.

The proposal also asks for six years of alimony at $1,500 per month, for a significant amount of child support, and for Bob to pay the full cost of both kids' Catholic-school tuition.

Bob is not surprised or upset by this proposal. He's focused on how we will respond. We are discussing strategy. He's fine with the child-support numbers proposed by his wife's lawyer and with paying the school tuition, but we both agree the asset division is tilted too far in his wife's favor and the alimony payments are too high and last too long. Based on my recommendation as to what the court would be likely to do, Bob is prepared to accept a 55/45 split of the assets in his wife's favor, which would leave him with a significantly lower cash payout on his interest in his company, and to pay five years of alimony at $1,200 per month. In order to get there, we decide to counteroffer with a 50/50 split and three years of alimony at $1,000 per month. He and I both know they'll come back with something a little lower than their original proposal, we'll respond with something higher than our counterproposal, the negotiation dance will play out, and presumably we'll close the gap near, if not precisely where, Bob wants to land.

Bob is making my job easy, because he understands that divorce is, at its essence, an economic transaction that needs to be negotiated just like any other deal. This attitude can't be attributed solely to his experience as a businessman who negotiates contracts, although that may be a factor. Like many men I represent in divorce cases, Bob is fundamentally comfortable with the idea that he will need to provide for his wife after they're no longer married, and he accepts that the assets they accumulated while they were together, paid for with his income from his business, are going to be shared with her. He's a provider and he takes pride in that. With clients like Bob, I sense that it's actually a mark of social status to be able to keep his family comfortable after a divorce. And this outlook is not the sole province of higher-income earners. I've represented housepainters, grocers, and landscapers who had the same attitude; in some cases there's almost a macho tinge to it. (Some divorce lawyers buy into this, too. Consider this whispered comment in the courthouse hallway after a custody hearing where opposing counsel, a kind of macho guy himself, who does criminal defense work as well as family law, told me, "My guy asked me if he could get alimony from your lady, and I told him, yeah, maybe, but don't be a pussy.")

It can be a different story with women. My women breadwinner clients are often upset that they have to share their savings accounts and 401(k)s with their husbands. And almost to a woman, they become apoplectic at the prospect of paying alimony. They generally feel that their underemployed or nonworking husbands were deadbeats and leeches and that they had to do everything: earn the money and take primary responsibility for the house and the kids. I tend to believe them on this second point, both from personal knowledge of how most families I know (including mine) operate and from the large body of research documenting the "second shift" worked at home by women who are also full-time members of the labor force. But the main difference from the Bob-type client is their attitude. These women are deeply disappointed that they married men who didn't carry their weight financially. I don't think that women grow up with the cultural expectation that we will be the main providers for our families, so we feel ripped off when we have to assume that role by default and then victimized by the divorce process.

I try to soften the blow by explaining to them the genesis of the modern divorce code, that property used to be divided solely by title in divorce cases and that this left most women, who had not been in the labor market and therefore had no savings or pensions, literally penniless. The contemporary view of divorce in this country, which is now embodied in the laws of every state, is that marriage is an economic partnership, and property acquired during marriage belongs to both people, regardless of who paid for it or whose name is on the deed or bank account or car title. These were feminist legal reforms of huge importance for the status of women in the twentieth century. It was a radical notion to recognize and validate the noneconomic contributions wives made in raising children and running households.

So, I tell my unhappy woman breadwinner client, these

laws were designed to protect women, but they're gender neutral. If your husband is the nonworking spouse, he's going to receive the same consideration you would if you were the homemaker. My unhappy woman breadwinner client might find this policy lecture interesting (I try), but it won't stop her from feeling screwed. And I totally get it. No question it's still a patriarchal world out there, it's still harder for women to get ahead in the workplace, and there's still a societal (and often internal) assumption that women will take on the lion's share of child care and household responsibilities. But as much as I empathize, I also sigh inside, because it's just so much more difficult to represent someone who's angry and who wants to talk to me about how unfair "the system" is. I've had that conversation so many times, arising in so many different contexts, and I know from experience that it's pointless. I'm not going to convince my resentful clients that the divorce laws are basically fair and reasonable and grounded in sound public policy (which I do believe), and they're not going to convince me that they are being victimized by an unfair "system." I'd way rather have the strategy conversation with Bob about different options for structuring his settlement, asset percentages, and the tax benefit of alimony.

REGARDLESS OF MY clients' varying attitudes about money, however, I have observed a palpable sense of relief in being able to discuss the particulars of their financial circumstances with me. It makes me wonder if money issues can be so damaging to marriages in part because of the taboo against talking to others about them. When a marriage is on the rocks, many people turn to friends and family for comfort and advice, disclosing and dissecting lurid details of affairs, abuse, and addiction, to name a few common marriage busters. But they do not tend to sit down with these supportive types to review bank statements, mortgage balances, or tax returns, to look at the financial structure they have to work with and decide how—and if—to reconfigure it if they get divorced. If we felt freer to talk about money the way we talk about everything else, maybe my clients would be able to think about these issues with less anxiety.

Legal Fiction

I was talking to a cousin of mine at a family gathering, and the dinner conversation turned to her adoption, as a girl, by her stepfather. My cousin's father died when she was very young and her mother remarried a man who adopted her. This sounds like a good thing, but the problem was that the marriage ultimately failed and he effectively ditched my cousin along with his wife in the divorce. Now in her forties, my cousin hasn't seen him since she was fifteen. We were discussing the perils of stepparent adoptions, and my cousin said she wished it had been explained to her at the time that as a result of the adoption she would receive an entirely new birth certificate with her adoptive father's name on it. The reality of her biological father was, effectively, wiped out—she had lost him to cancer before she could ever get to know him, and then his very existence as her father on the day she was born was erased and replaced by a man who apparently considered her part of the package of a marriage, which didn't last, rather than a lifetime commitment.

People at the dinner table were astonished to learn that birth certificates are altered in adoptions. I share their astonishment. I was shocked by this practice the first time I handled an adoption. It seems so odd and so completely unlegalistic: the intentional creation, by judicial decree, of a false document. It is not called an "adoption certificate"; it is called a "birth certificate," and it's a back-dated, official "birth" record, which contains the names of two parents, at least one of whom was not in fact the parent at the time of the child's birth.

Who are we kidding? What interests do we serve by issuing these phony documents? You can be prosecuted for using a fake ID at a bar when you're nineteen, but somehow courts can wipe out one identity and replace it with a new one with the stroke of a pen. I recognize that this practice is based on the intense privacy and secrecy that has historically surrounded adoption, but today it seems uncomfortably reminiscent of actions taken in the shadows of a totalitarian regime. The obliteration of an identity, the rewriting of a personal history. And the results can be, frankly, ludicrous. If a gay couple adopts a child, a birth certificate will be issued with the names of both dads or both moms. If a child is adopted by Americans in Guatemala, for instance, and goes through a U.S. readoption after she moves here, the birth certificate names only her adoptive American parents, with the location of her birth listed as the United States.

The same goes for name changes, with the end result being a new birth certificate. Think about this in the context of transgendered people, who routinely seek judicial name changes. You were born with a boy's body. Later in life you begin living as a woman; you may or may not have sex reassignment surgery, but regardless, you officially become, to the world at large, female rather than male. Reasonably, you want to change your name to match the gender you inhabit, and the court will entertain and grant those requests. The order changing your name will then be the basis for authorizing the appropriate government agency to issue a new birth certificate with that name and gender. In an instant, the past is completely altered.

It's complicated, though. Transgendered clients I have represented in name-change actions desperately want and need those new birth certificates. To change your name with Social Security, to get a new driver's license, to apply for a passport: It all goes back to the birth certificate. And certainly a transgendered person's privacy should be protected; she shouldn't constantly have to explain to potential employers or the clerk at the Department of Motor Vehicles that her name used to be William because she used to be considered a guy. There has got to be a better solution, an official document that is what it says it is, rather than certifying a lie.

THERE ARE OTHER areas of the law that create and maintain fictions, where social policy is carried out in disregard of science and history. The big one in family law is the presumption of paternity. This ancient common-law doctrine, alive and well in Pennsylvania, provides that a child born to a married woman is presumed to be the child of her husband. This translates into scenarios where biological fathers can be foreclosed from having any legal recourse to form relationships with their children, and men who raise children to whom they are not biologically related can be obligated to support them through their entire childhood.

Here's how it can play out. A married woman has an affair and gets pregnant. Husband or boyfriend could be the father. Baby boy is born. A couple of years down the road, boyfriend (probably now ex-boyfriend) decides he wants to have a relationship with baby boy. Mother won't speak to him, so he files a petition for DNA testing to try to establish that baby boy is in fact his offspring. He's out of luck. The court will not interfere with the intact family, that is, husband, wife, and baby boy who was born during their marriage. The law prevents this testing in favor of upholding the presumption that the husband is the father.

This certainly seems at odds with the modern world. But

what *is* a father? Isn't that really the question this presumption is designed to address? Courts and legislatures have wrestled with this question for centuries. It used to be that paternity was a lot harder to definitively establish. With DNA testing, it's a whole different ball game; the science is cheap and easy and accurate (all it takes is a kit from the drugstore and a couple of Q-tips). We can tell who the biological father is. Now the question becomes stark: Should we? Does it benefit the child? Baby boy knows husband as his father. What social benefit is served in disrupting that comfortable fiction by allowing another man—who has not been raising him—to establish their genetic connection? Maybe husband will reject baby boy, especially if he and mother divorce. Maybe (really, certainly) baby boy's world will be rocked disastrously by learning that the man he thought was his father, and who has cared for him as a father, is not. From baby boy's perspective, the fiction makes sense.

Here's the other way it plays out. Assume same family configuration, except that mother and husband are divorced and husband is paying child support for baby boy. Boyfriend is not in the picture. Husband, who at this point knows about boyfriend, decides to find out the truth about baby boy's paternity, so he does DNA testing on himself and baby boy and learns that they are not genetically related. Husband files a petition to stop paying child support and to have boyfriend submit to DNA testing to establish that boyfriend is the father and so should be the one to pay child support. Husband is out of luck: The court will not permit this. He and mother were married when baby boy was born and he assumed responsibility for the child. So even though he and mother are divorced, he is still the legal father and will have to continue to support baby boy. The court will not allow him to haul boyfriend into court and make him submit to DNA testing. And what about baby boy in this scenario? Will husband reject him?

THIS MAY SEEM to be a fiction of the same magnitude as the birth certificates. But I don't think so. There is a clear upside here. The goal is to protect children at the expense of the adults in their lives who made a mess of things. It provides them with stability and support. It is also based on the recognition that a father is more than a sperm donor. On the downside, though, it is certainly a policy based on the notion that government knows best, that government will go so far as to deny us access to essential knowledge about ourselves and our children on the assumption that they will be better off if we go without it. In that way it is similar to the new "birth" certificates. So while I am sympathetic to the social policies behind the presumption of paternity, ultimately I think it's a bad idea for government to be in the business of mandating that certain secrets be kept. All families, in all their variety, are worthy of legal recognition and protection, not just the ones that conform to traditional norms.

Beth/Hearsay

Since Beth is the parent who initiated the custody action, we put our case on first. Meaning we start with our witnesses. Judge Diamond allotted only one day for the trial; we're scheduled to start at 9 a.m. and I'm sure he'll cut us off by 5:00. That's our window. I plan to call Beth and Marla Peres, the preschool teacher, and to ask the judge to interview Kaitlyn and Jimmy in chambers. Beth will be my main witness. I'll have her testify about the general custody topics; I want to establish that she has historically been the children's primary caretaker, that it is she who has fed and clothed and bathed them, that she bought the school supplies, supervised the homework, volunteered in the classroom, made the doctors' appointments, and cared for them when they were sick. I can't have her testify that Brian isn't capable of this type of hands-on parenting, because he's never had the opportunity to do it. And, despite her initial concerns about meals and bedtimes and getting to school on time, Brian seems to have stepped up to the plate in those areas. After the first few visits, Beth could not honestly say that when the kids returned home, they were hungry or tired or that Kaitlyn's schoolwork wasn't done. So our focus on these topics has to be positive, rather than negative: specifically, that Beth is a great parent, that the children have thrived under her care, and that the court shouldn't rock the boat.

Then there's the abuse. That's where this case veers off in a different, and far more serious, direction. I plan to ask Beth about her discovery of the bruise, about Brian's past abuse of her, about the incident when Brian tied Jimmy to the chair and force-fed him, and about Jimmy's spontaneous disclosure that night in the bathtub. I will have her identify the photographs of Jimmy's bruised arm and we'll offer those into evidence during her testimony.

I have one major evidentiary concern. While Beth's testimony about the bruise and about Brian's actions toward her and Jimmy is admissible, since it consists of her description of what she herself saw and heard, asking her to recount what Jimmy told her when he was in the bathtub is different. It's a request for hearsay, an "out of court statement offered for the truth of the matter stated." (Aside on rules of evidence: an "out of court statement" is inadmissible only if a witness is being asked to testify about what another person said in order to establish that the person's statement is true, in other words, that Brian did in fact intentionally squeeze Jimmy's arm. However, if all Jimmy had said to Beth was "I don't like Daddy," I would expect a hearsay objection to be overruled, because the purpose for which I would be offering that testimony to the court would be to show how Jimmy feels about his dad, not to prove that Brian isn't likeable. It would be evidence about Jimmy, which Beth could describe because she had the conversation with Jimmy, rather than evidence about Brian, which the court would be hearing secondhand from Beth.)

I don't know which way Judge Diamond will roll on this. If it were a car accident case, I would never even consider asking Beth to testify about what a person who saw the crash told her about how it happened. That would be inadmissible hearsay, and it would be professionally embarrassing even to ask such a question; that's Evidence 101. (Here's the totally predictable script: Me: "Did Louise see the accident too?" Beth: "Yes." Me: "What did she tell you about it?" Opposing counsel: "Objection! Calls for hearsay." Judge: "Objection sustained. Next question.")

But custody cases are different. When young children are involved, some judges permit parents and other adults who care for them to testify about what the children said to them regarding matters of importance to the case, such as events that happened in the other parent's home. If you were rushing straight from the bar exam into court to try a custody case, you would be perplexed by this, because there's nothing in my state's rules of evidence that creates an exception to the rule against hearsay for the statements of children in child custody cases. But many judges admit them anyway. Custody cases are heard without juries, and I think some judges feel that they will be able to apply the appropriate degree of skepticism to the testimony, knowing that it is coming to them secondhand and has a built-in bias because it serves the interest of the party presenting it. They'll be able to give the testimony, in legal parlance, "the appropriate weight."

I call a lawyer I know who practices exclusively in the county where this case is being heard, and I ask if he knows Judge Diamond's take on this issue. He doesn't, but he tells me the judge is pretty old school and likely to be on the strict-application-of-the-rules side. Of course, none of this is going to matter if Jimmy tells the judge himself. In that case, I don't need Beth to report on it. But I think that is unlikely. Our request to suspend Brian's visits is going to hinge on one specific fact—whether Brian intentionally squeezed Jimmy's arm—and I am sure Judge Diamond will want to interview Jimmy. But I'm anticipating that he won't get much out of it. After all, Jimmy didn't tell his own mother for over a week, he didn't tell the doctor, and he didn't tell the Child Protective Services caseworker, who probably spent way longer talking to him than the judge will and certainly has more training in interviewing children.

I ARRIVE AT court a little before 9 a.m. There's a woman with a file in her lap sitting in the hallway; she must be the caseworker from CPS, subpoenaed by Brian's lawyer. Beth and two women I've never met are standing near the water fountain, talking to a young boy and girl who've got to be Jimmy and Kaitlyn. I assume the dressed-up woman is Marla Peres, with whom I've only spoken on the phone, and the other, an older version of Beth in jeans and sneakers, is her sister, who's come to wait outside the courtroom with the kids until the judge calls them. I take Beth into the courtroom. Brian and his lawyer, Francis, are already seated at counsel table, waiting. We check in and sit down. Judge Diamond takes the bench, looking rushed and irritated. A bit alarming, I think, given that the day is just starting.

I call Beth to the stand and start with the background: where she and Brian live, when they separated, how old their kids are, where they attend school, what the temporary custody order is. I move into a detailed narrative of her role in the kids' lives, essentially a job description of the life of a stay-at-home mom who's good at her work. I have her describe her children, their personalities, what makes them happy, what makes them sad, what they're good at, what frustrates and concerns them. She knows to include a specific description of Jimmy's high level of activity and his propensity to break things. None of this is controversial and all goes smoothly. No objections from Francis. I shift gears and begin a line of questioning about Brian's treatment of her. I have Beth describe Brian slapping and pinching her. I establish that the children were in the house when these incidents took place, but I don't ask if they witnessed the fights. Despite what Beth initially told me, when I was prepping her testimony it turned out that she didn't actually know if the children saw any of these incidents, and we concluded that, in fact, they probably didn't because Brian's rampages usually occurred late at night when the children were asleep.

As I start to have her describe the plate-throwing incident, Judge Diamond interrupts me. "Ms. Klaw, we have limited time today. I realize that the court has an obligation to consider this evidence and I will certainly do so, but if I understand correctly, these incidents your client is testifying about happened quite some time ago and did not involve the children. Therefore, I would suggest you do not use up more time on this topic. This is a custody case and my focus, as you know, is the children. So I suggest you move on." I don't argue with him. I'm pleased he heard the amount he permitted; I figure it sets up a picture of Brian as someone other than the charming concerned father he will surely appear to be when he testifies later today.

I move to the tying-to-the-chair/force-feeding incident. That, the judge allows me to question Beth about in detail, and he takes copious notes. Beth is doing well. She describes Brian becoming more and more aggravated as Jimmy resisted, and literally shoving pieces of chicken into his mouth, which Jimmy couldn't even swallow because, she says, he was crying so hard. I can see Brian, out of the corner of my eye, shaking his head in a silent "no" during this testimony.

We continue to the discovery of the bruise. I have Beth identify the photographs and I move them into evidence. Now we hit up against the first hearsay issue involving Jimmy. I would like to ask Beth, Did you ask Jimmy how he got the bruise? Her answer would be yes, and then I would follow up with, What did he tell you? That question, though, would generate a hearsay objection from Francis, and we'd end up having the argument over the admissibility of Jimmy's statements earlier than I want to have it. I want the judge to hear more. I want to move further into the narrative to draw him in, maybe make him more sympathetic, or curious, or whatever (he's human, after all), so he's more likely to allow Beth to testify to what Jimmy said later in the bathtub, the really important part. So I do the standard end run to avoid a hearsay objection:

"Did you ask Jimmy how he got the bruise?"

"Yes"

"As a result of that conversation, what, if anything, did you do next?"

"I called Jimmy's dad."

That's beautiful. Actually, the implication is that Jimmy might have fingered Brian right then, but there are no grounds for an objection. And I can have Beth testify about what Brian said during that conversation. Statements the other party made directly to my witness are not considered hearsay. (That's called "admission of a party opponent.")

"What did Mr. Foster say?"

"He said, yeah, he saw it, he had no idea how Jimmy got it but probably it was from something at school or Kaitlyn did it. He got very annoyed with me and started yelling that it was just a bruise and Jimmy was fine and as usual I was being ridiculous."

Clear sailing, so far. We move on through the meeting with the preschool teacher, the CPS investigation, and the forensic pediatric exam. I ask Beth about the outcome of the investigation so that the judge knows it was unfounded but he hears it first from us. Then I move to the heart of her testimony.

"At some time after the CPS investigation, did you learn how Jimmy got the bruise?"

"Yes."

"How?"

Beth starts to describe the scene, the evening bath, the little boy playing with the tugboat, the tilted head, his looking up at her. "And all of a sudden, he says to me —" Francis jumps to his feet. "Objection. Calls for hearsay."

"Counsel?" Judge Diamond swivels his head in my direction, looking for a response.

I pull out every argument I can. That the statements I'm seeking to elicit fall into the category of either an "excited utterance" or a "present sense impression," both of which are exceptions to the hearsay rule. That the child is barely five years old, so the policy behind the hearsay rule, which is to ensure reliability of the out-of-court statements, isn't served here. That this is a custody case; that the child is here to be interviewed; and that he (the judge) shouldn't exclude this important testimony from the mother because it's all part of the puzzle, and can, instead, decide what weight to give it after he's heard the whole case. All these arguments are weak. It comes down to whether the judge insists on going by the book, in which case he should exclude the testimony. And Francis is playing to that. He responds very forcefully, telling His Honor that my arguments are totally inapplicable and that this is classic hearsay, not subject to any exception in the rules of evidence. He says it would be a gross miscarriage of justice to permit my client to testify to alleged statements made by the child that would be offered specifically to prove that his client committed child abuse. The child is here, he tells the judge, you can ask *him* what happened to his arm.

Judge Diamond listens politely to both of us. When Francis finishes, and I open my mouth to begin some form of rebuttal, he cuts me off. "Ms. Klaw, there is no applicable exception to the hearsay rule. Objection sustained. Move on."

Although I did have the "hearsay conversation" with Beth, several times, in fact, she looks shocked. Maybe it didn't sink in. This was to be the climax of her testimony,

and I can tell by the look on her face what she's thinking: How could the judge not want to hear what my son
told me? He's only five! And his father threatened him! Of
course he didn't tell the social worker or his teacher. And I
would never make this up. I'm just doing what any mother
would do, trying to protect her child.

I regroup and bring her testimony to a close. I have her
describe how long the bruise lasted. I ask her if Jimmy ever
had a bruise anything like this one (no, of course.) I go
back over the custody schedule in more detail to make it
clear that this could only have happened between the time
Jimmy left school on Wednesday with his father and the
time she picked him up the following Thursday afternoon.
My thought is to bring the judge's attention back to the se-
verity of the injury, how unlikely it was to have been caused
accidentally, and that we know for sure that Beth discovered it immediately following a period in which Brian had
custody of Jimmy. I conclude, "No more questions," and
sit down.

Judge Diamond looks at Francis. "Cross-examination."

Francis starts right in, picking up on my last questions.

"Ms. Foster, the bruise occurred during a time period
Brian had Jimmy in his custody. So that means you weren't
there, were you?"

"No, I wasn't."

"So you would agree you have no firsthand knowledge
of what happened, do you?"

"Well, I didn't see it happening, if that's what you mean."

"And you took Jimmy for a forensic exam with a pediatrician who specializes in evaluating children who've been abused, right?"

"I took him to the doctor the CPS lady, Ms. Williams, told me to, yes. But Jimmy didn't tell him anything."

"And that doctor thoroughly examined Jimmy, didn't he?"

"Yes, but Jimmy didn't tell him anything."

"And the doctor could not say that this injury was caused intentionally, could he?

"No."

"In fact, his records show there were no handprints or fingerprints, don't they?"

"I don't know."

"So as far as he could tell, it could be accidental, correct?"

"I guess so."

"The social worker for Child Protective Services, Ms. Williams, came to your house, correct?"

"Yes."

"She interviewed you and Jimmy and your daughter, Kaitlyn, didn't she?"

"Yes, but Jimmy didn't tell her anything."

"She's specifically trained to investigate allegations of child abuse, isn't she?"

"I don't know; I guess so."

"She completed her investigation and concluded that the allegations of abuse were unfounded, didn't she?"

"Yes, because Jimmy wouldn't talk to her."

"And she closed the case, correct?"

"Yes."

"So, you would agree, then, that two professionals in the field of child abuse investigation, the pediatrician from Children's Hospital and Ms. Williams, were unable to conclude that this bruise was intentionally caused by my client?"

"Yes, because Jimmy didn't tell them what happened."

"And yet you persist in your belief that your husband caused this bruise."

"Yes—because that's what my son told me and I believe my son."

"Move to strike, Your Honor. You sustained my objection regarding statements of the child."

I can't argue with that. Francis is correct. Judge Diamond looks at the court reporter and instructs her to strike (remove) the answer from the record. Then he turns toward the witness stand and speaks rather sternly to Beth. "Ms. Foster, I have already ruled on this matter. I will remind you that you may not testify about statements your child allegedly made to you. Do you understand?"

"Yes, Your Honor." Beth's eyes are filled with tears. I have that helpless feeling I often get during my adversary's cross of my client; the questions aren't improper, so I can't object to them, yet I can see my client starting to fall apart on the stand. Sometimes I object anyway, just to break up the flow, to show my client I'm standing up for her, but that's risky because it can annoy the judge. Francis is very skilled; he isn't badgering her (that would be something I could legitimately object to), and his questions are textbook cross-examination: narrow and limited, revealing his client's version of the story through the questions themselves. Beth's answers are incidental. And I know what's coming next.

"You're angry with my client, aren't you?"

"No."

This is the perfect example of a question on cross where the answer doesn't matter at all. Francis makes his point either way. Of course she's mad at Brian. She just testified he abused her and she believes he's abused her child. So she can admit it, but that would mean she's agreeing that she has a bias against Brian, which could cast doubt about the accuracy of her testimony. If she denies it, as she just did, she's not believable.

"He moved out shortly after you discovered he was having an affair, didn't he?"

"Yes, but that's not why he moved out."

Francis keeps on going. It doesn't matter why Brian moved out and he doesn't need to give Beth an opportunity to explain it.

"And you told him he would pay for what he'd done to you, didn't you?"

"I never said that."

Again, the answer doesn't matter. Even if she didn't say

that, he's made his point: She has a motive to lie. This whole thing could be payback.

"And these allegations about your son's bruise were made by you less than three weeks before this trial, were they not?"

"Yes, because that's when I saw the bruise."

"If this court suspends my client's visits with his children, you certainly would have paid him back for the affair, wouldn't you?"

"Objection," I say, as I rise. "Argumentative."

Judge Diamond nods and appears to be about to admonish Francis, but Francis preempts him. "I'll withdraw the question, Your Honor." He knows he's made his point. He looks at his notes briefly, looks back up at the judge, and puts down his legal pad. "No further questions."

Marla/Neutral Witness

After Beth steps down and retakes her seat next to me at counsel table, I call Marla Peres. I subpoenaed Jimmy's preschool teacher for three reasons. The first is to establish that the injury did not occur at school, the second is to have her describe what the bruise looked like when she saw it on the Friday morning after Beth discovered it, and the third is to tell the court about the morning she saw Brian speaking harshly to Jimmy. The first point needs to be part of the record and she's the only witness who can testify to it. The second point has already come in through Beth and the photographs, but I'd like to have a third party—not a parent—describe the bruise, as well, in order to emphasize how severe it was. The third point bolsters Beth's testimony that Brian has been abusive to Jimmy in the recent past, and it contradicts the testimony I'm expecting from Brian that he's a model dad.

Unlike most witnesses in custody cases, who are inherently biased because they're family members or close friends, teachers are by definition neutral, so what they say tends to carry a lot of weight with the court. Understandably, they (like most everybody else) hate being subpoenaed, so I try to do so only if it's absolutely necessary.

Marla has become quite friendly with Beth. Marla's a young mom with two small children of her own. She clearly isn't too fond of Brian, so she doesn't seem to mind testifying. My experience with teachers is that they don't tend to do well in the adversarial environment of a courtroom. It's so foreign to them, especially to a preschool teacher. Marla spends her days teaching collaboration and kindness. Everything at preschool is supposed to be kind and fair and fun—a far cry from family court. So I did my best to prep her thoroughly during a phone conversation, making sure she's definitive enough in her statements about what she observed, even if challenged on cross, and that she doesn't inadvertently say anything that might show an affinity for Beth or distaste for Brian, either of which could lessen the impact of her testimony.

Marla, along with Ms. Williams, has been out in the hallway during Beth's testimony. Witnesses are not allowed to hear the testimony of other witnesses, except for the parties to the case, who are present for the entire trial. A court officer brings Marla in and she takes the stand. She is dressed for the occasion in a black suit, her dark hair loose and curly around her face. I start with background. How long she's worked at the preschool (six years), and how long she's known Jimmy (two years, because she moved up to be a teacher in the oldest class this year at the same time he did). We establish the time frame. On Wednesday, February 22, Beth took Jimmy to school as usual. Marla is sure he did not have a bruise on his arm that day, because a gymnastics instructor comes into her class on Wednesday afternoons to teach tumbling, and the kids all put on T-shirts given to them by the gymnastics school. If Jimmy had had the bruise then, she would definitely have seen it. She's sure of that, because when Beth showed her the bruise the following Friday morning, it covered Jimmy's whole upper right arm, from his shoulder down to his elbow, so it would have been clearly visible when Jimmy was wearing a T-shirt. And no, Jimmy did not have any kind of accident during tumbling; she was right there watching, because she assists the instructor during class.

Marla confirmed that Brian picked Jimmy up from school on Wednesday after tumbling and brought him back the following morning, Thursday, the 23rd. She did not see his arm that day because he was wearing a sweatshirt. She knows Jimmy was wearing it because he had recently become obsessed with a particular Spiderman hoodie. He had been wearing it to school every day for the last couple of weeks, and she and Jimmy had joked about it. That Thursday, Beth picked Jimmy up at the usual time. I moved to Friday morning. I asked Marla to describe Jimmy's arm and explain why she called Child Protective Services.

No fireworks, no objections. The court officer is picking at a loose button on his jacket. I can see Judge Diamond suppressing a yawn.

"What time do you get to school?"

"We open at seven thirty, so I have to be there by seven fifteen."

"Do you see Jimmy in the mornings when he's dropped off?"

"Yes. His mom drops him off by eight. Now his dad drops him off on Thursdays, and he brings him a little later. But I'm always there."

"Could you describe how Jimmy typically behaves when he's dropped off?"

"Sure. Jimmy loves school. He runs into the classroom to say hi to me and his friends. He's so excited that his mom has to remind him a couple of times to put his jacket and his lunch in his cubby. He just wants to start playing right away."

"Does he act that way no matter which parent brings him to school?"

"Usually, but about a month ago, one of the days his dad brought him in he was crying."

"Can you describe what you saw that day?"

"Jimmy's dad brought him to school, and Jimmy stayed out in the hallway instead of running into the classroom like he usually does. And I heard him crying."

"Could you see him in the hallway?"

"Yes."

"What was he doing?"

"He was crying and his dad was trying to get him into the room but he wouldn't come. And his dad was talking to him, like, in a very loud whisper."

"Did you hear what Mr. Foster was saying?"

"No. But Jimmy started to cry louder."

"Did Jimmy eventually come into the classroom?"

"Yes."

"What was Mr. Foster doing when Jimmy came in?"

"He sort of dumped Jimmy's jacket and his lunchbox on a table, instead of taking them to his cubby. And then he just turned around and left, without saying good-bye or anything."

"Ms. Peres, have you ever seen Jimmy crying when his mother drops him off at school?"

"No."

We're done. I've gotten all I can from this witness, and I'm hoping she was helpful. I thank Marla for her time. Francis's cross-examination of Marla is brief and gentle, as it should be. There's no benefit to bullying a preschool teacher; that would just make the judge feel sympathy for her. And if Francis asks her lots of questions, he might open the door for her to say something else damaging about Brian. He asks Marla if some children cry when their parents drop them off at preschool, and if some children go through an adjustment period when their parents separate.

Yes, of course, she answers to both questions. He doesn't challenge her on her testimony that the injury could not have occurred at school on the Thursday in question. He simply points out that she didn't see the bruise until Friday morning, and that Jimmy had been picked up from school the day before by his mother. So it's possible that the accident (as he calls it) could have happened at Beth's house on Thursday night; she has no way of knowing, right? That's right, Marla says; I wasn't there.

After Marla's testimony is finished and Judge Diamond has excused her from the courtroom, he asks me if we have any other witnesses.

Just the children, I tell him; they're waiting in the hallway with my client's sister, ready whenever the court wishes to interview them.

"My practice in custody cases is to interview children at the conclusion of the case. And we are going to finish today, as you know. So I am going to set aside an hour at the end of the day for those interviews. Other than the children, Ms. Klaw, do you rest your case?"

"We rest, Your Honor."

"Very good. We'll break for lunch and resume at one fifteen p.m. with Mr. DiLorenzo's first witness. Court is in recess."

Divorce Equality

The other day, a woman who wants a divorce called me. Which initially sounded fine, since that's what I do. But upon further discussion, it turned out not to be fine. It turned out that I can't get her divorced, and neither can anyone else. She's stuck in a marriage that she and her spouse both want to end, with no feasible way out.

Sound like the eighteenth century? Or Saudi Arabia, perhaps? To the contrary, this woman suffers from a thoroughly modern problem. The problem is that her spouse is a wife, not a husband. This woman married her partner in Vermont—picture the quaint inn, the rolling green hills dotted with black-and-white cows, the wedding package so appealing to same-sex couples in that most progressive state of all—and after the wedding, they packed up and drove back home to Philly. Therein lies the problem. Pennsylvania does not recognize their marriage as valid, thanks to our state's version of the federal Defense of Marriage Act. Not only does this law, passed by a group of homophobic legislators in Harrisburg back in 1996, prohibit same-sex marriage here, it also provides that such a marriage entered into in another state is "void in this Commonwealth." And if Pennsylvania doesn't recognize you as being married in the first place, its courts have no authority to divorce you.

You'd think I would just tell my would-be client to go back to Vermont to get divorced. But she can't. Because although Vermont welcomes nonresidents into the state to marry, the opposite is true when it comes to divorce: You have to live there. And this is not unique to Vermont; it's the case across the country. There is no state that requires residency as a prerequisite for a marriage license. You can drive to Vegas from anywhere at all and get married in the Elvis Chapel. Which is why gay and lesbian couples have flooded into Vermont and Massachusetts and New Hampshire and the rest of the states where they can legally marry—for the weekend, that is. Like Vermont, however, all states currently require that at least one spouse be a resident in order to file for divorce. While "residency" is defined differently by different states, it always means that at least one of the spouses has to live there for some defined period of time (in the case of Vermont, for six months) before a divorce complaint can be filed. I assume that the rationale behind these divorce residency requirements is that states don't want to tie up their court systems adjudicating divorces for people who don't actually live (or pay taxes) there.

What's my would-be client to do? She's stuck, unless she

or her wife (a) move to a state that will recognize their marriage and (b) live there long enough to satisfy the residency requirement so they can file for divorce. And if they don't do this and one of them wants to marry someone else? She can't. Because she's still married. The irony is overwhelming. Gay people are fighting so hard for marriage equality, and now, when some of those marriages don't work out (what a surprise; they're no different from straight people!), they also need to fight for the right to divorce.

So my Vermont-married, would-be client, and all those in similar circumstances, have no access to the courts to get divorced. The related, and far more common, would-be client is the *un*married gay person whose long-term, marriage-like relationship ends. Can he avail himself of the remedies available to married people under our divorce laws? Is she entitled to any assets or support from her ex?

That's the question I was asked by Eddie, who'd been in a relationship for twenty-two years when his partner dumped him for another man. Older, educated, and successful, Marco, the ex, owned a house, investments, and a pension. Eddie had none of those. He was a high school graduate who essentially hadn't worked since he moved in with Marco at the age of twenty-one. He dabbled in various artistic pursuits, none of them profitable. But that was okay, because Marco supported him and, according to Eddie, specifically, explicitly, told him that he always would. So Eddie enjoyed their comfortable, middle-class life together, and never took any measures to ensure his own financial security. When Marco ended the relationship, Eddie was faced with the hard reality that here he was, forty-three years old, with no money in the bank and no ability to earn much more than minimum wage. He came to me to find out if the promises Marco made could be enforced.

I looked into it and saw that the answer was a resounding maybe. It's fairly uncharted territory in Pennsylvania. In addition to same-sex couples not having the protection of our divorce code, since they can neither marry here nor have their out-of-state marriages recognized, we have no civil-union or domestic-partnership laws either. Which is why my client Jorani was better off marrying her boyfriend, even with a restrictive prenuptial agreement, than simply continuing to live with him. What we're left with is the common law, those basic legal principles brought over from England centuries ago. For Eddie, the common law principle on which we could hang our hat was the law of contracts. We would have to convince a judge that Eddie and Marco had made a contract that Marco breached, and as a result, Eddie was entitled to compensation. This would not be an easy task, since there was no written agreement. Our argument would be that the existence of a contract could be implied from Eddie's and Marco's words and actions.

Not surprisingly, Marco denied that he made any such promises to Eddie, and he downplayed the seriousness of the relationship, emphasizing both men's admission to having had other sexual partners during the decades they lived together. At trial, Eddie testified about specific instances in which Marco told him he would provide for Eddie financially for the rest of his life, and we presented evidence of actions taken by Marco that would support that testimony, such as naming Eddie the beneficiary of his pension and his life insurance and providing for Eddie in his will.

A contract requires an offer and an acceptance. We argued to the judge that Marco offered to Eddie, by his verbal promises and by his conduct, which was consistent with those promises, that he would take care of Eddie forever. Eddie, we said, in order to provide companionship and domestic services to Marco, accepted that offer by not pursuing education or career opportunities. The tricky thing about this argument is we had to show that "companionship and domestic services" was really that, rather than sexual services, as the courts won't enforce such a contract. Just like you can't sue to enforce a drug deal gone bad or to recoup the amount you were shorted in an extortion scheme, you can't look to the courts to enforce a contract for, essentially, prostitution.

There was little case law to rely on in Pennsylvania, but we found some very helpful decisions coming from our sister state across the Delaware River. The New Jersey Supreme Court, in a case involving an unmarried heterosexual couple (actually, one party, Mr. Roccamonte, was married, but to someone else, but the claim for support was brought against his estate after his death by his girlfriend, with whom he had lived for twenty-five years), held that "a general promise of support for life, broadly expressed, made by one party to the other with some form of consideration given by the other will suffice to form a contract."

"Consideration" refers to what is given in exchange for a promise. If there's no consideration, a promise just becomes a gift, and you can't force someone to give you a gift. But if Mr. Roccamonte promised his girlfriend financial support in exchange for housekeeping services, and the housekeeping services were in fact performed by her, then there is consideration for his promise of support—called by the wonderful name "palimony" in New Jersey and in many other courts around the country—and he can be required to provide it. That is, so long as the consideration is not sex.

In the *Roccamonte* case, the New Jersey Supreme Court found that the plaintiff's "making a home for the defendant, cooking for him, and acting as his social companion" was ample consideration in exchange for Mr. Roccamonte's promise to support her for life. The court stated that the law of New Jersey was that "unmarried adult partners, even those who may be married to others, have the right to choose to cohabit together in a marital-like relationship, and that if one of those partners is induced to do so by a promise of support given her by the other, that promise will be enforced by the court."

We loved the *Roccamonte* case. We briefed it thoroughly

for the judge. Unfortunately, what the New Jersey Supreme Court rules is not binding on the courts of Pennsylvania; it's merely illustrative. Given the dearth of law on the subject in our state, we asked the judge to look to New Jersey for guidance about how she should rule. Although we knew going in that it was a long shot, we were cautiously optimistic by the end of the trial. We felt that the judge had paid close attention to the testimony and seemed sympathetic to our client's plight. I made our pitch during closing arguments, asking her to award Eddie $300,000, which was the amount Marco received from the sale of the house where he and Eddie had lived for twenty-two years and Eddie had come to think of as his own. We argued that this was a reasonable amount to fulfill the promise of lifetime support, as it would enable Eddie to buy his own house. The judge nodded as she listened. My associate and I packed up our files and went back to the office, chewed our nails, and waited for her decision.

It came two weeks later. We lost. We never got out of the starting gate. The judge ruled that she could not find there was a contract. We had not convinced her, by a preponderance of the evidence, that Marco had in fact promised to provide for Eddie financially. So she never reached the legal issues, although her opinion indicates that had she done so, she actually would have been persuaded by our arguments. Had she found that a contract existed, she would have relied on *Roccamonte* and other cases we cited from

New Jersey, and she would have awarded money damages to Eddie. That's encouraging and useful in the long march forward to make good law for gay people in Pennsylvania, but it was of no help to Eddie. My whole firm was devastated, and Eddie just couldn't understand the result. It was so hard for him to accept that the judge believed Marco's version of events and not his.

We keep in touch. Eddie stops by the office now and then. He's working really hard at rebuilding his life, one step at a time. I can't help thinking, though, how much better off he'd be now if he and Marco had been able to marry. It would have been a garden variety divorce. By my calculation, Eddie would have walked away with at least half a million dollars in assets and he'd surely be receiving alimony, and there would have been no threshold legal hurdle to jump over; he would have been entitled to those remedies.

It's a great civil rights victory that at least some states have legalized same-sex marriage. But part of the benefit of marriage should be the legal protection afforded by divorce laws, based on our societal consensus that marriage is an economic partnership and that when it ends, what's been accumulated together should be fairly divided, regardless of title, and a spouse who was dependent on the other spouse's income during the marriage should be supported for some period of time afterward while he gets back on his feet. These are general principles embodied, to a greater or lesser degree, in the divorce laws of all fifty states. And if you are gay and have the misfortune to live in a state where you can't marry, or where your out-of-state marriage isn't recognized, you don't qualify for these basic protections. You could get lucky and win a case like Eddie's based on common-law contract principles, but it's an expensive, uphill battle. It's not the solution. Marriage equality won't be complete without divorce equality.

Opposing Counsel

Lawyers aren't allowed to communicate directly with the opposing party in a case if that person is represented by counsel. It's prohibited by our rules of professional conduct (Rule 4.2, to be exact). Sometimes it's very frustrating. Like yesterday. Around 6:30 on a hot Friday evening in August, while I was walking back from the creek with my wet dog and thinking about ushering in the weekend in the backyard with my husband and a gin and tonic, I got a call from a client, Gerri, who was outside the front door of her house with her soon-to-be-ex-husband. Problem was that the soon-to-be ex, Jason, was living there, and she was temporarily staying at a place almost two hours away and had become tired of the commute to her job and of schlepping their three young kids back and forth. She wanted to move back in until she could find permanent housing closer to their neighborhood. Jason, who had just recently moved his new girlfriend, her kids, and at least one pit bull into the house, not only didn't think this was such a good idea (understandable) but also told Gerri that she was not allowed to enter the house at all, much less live there. While this may have made sense from an emotional perspective, it was not legally supportable. The house still belonged to both of them and there was no order giving either one of them "exclusive possession."

Apparently Jason had called the police, who had come, shrugged, gotten back into their car, and driven away, since there was nothing they could do. That left Gerri and Jason, on the front porch, at an impasse.

None of this was a surprise, because two hours earlier I had been on the phone with Jason's lawyer, filling her in on Gerri's intentions. (Disclaimer: I didn't suggest the move-back-in plan to Gerri. I didn't have high hopes that imposing the blended family model on Jason, to say nothing of his new girlfriend, whom Gerri hadn't even met, had much chance of success. In fact, I thought it was a terrible idea. But Gerri had made up her mind and I wasn't able to talk her out of it, so my job was to back her up.)

Jason's lawyer was not happy. In fact she was so not happy that she was screaming. At me. She was screaming about how my client was not "allowed" to move in; how she would be filing an emergency petition Right Now (not much of a threat, since the chances of reaching a judge at 4:30 p.m. on a Friday in August are practically nonexistent, and anyway, there was no emergency); how she would be advising Jason not to turn over the children to Gerri (also not of much concern, since they were all going to be in the same house); and how she would be advising him to call the police. She also threw in many, shall we say, highly unflattering remarks about my client. Weirdly, at the same time as she was yelling at me about all this, I realized that she was also picking her kids up from camp. The conversation went something like this: "Yell, Yell, Yell—I'm going to file an emergency petition—Yell, Yell—Where are Michael and Sophie? Have you seen them? Thank you—and your client won't be able to take those kids anywhere—Yell, Yell, Yell. . . ."

When Gerri called me, dashing my hopes of having a peaceful cocktail anytime soon, she told me that she and Jason were sitting on the porch drinking iced tea and arguing about what to do. I liked this picture. I could work with this. I suggested that the two of them try to figure out some acceptable arrangement for sharing the house for a finite period of time. Jason grabbed the phone and started talking to me. Much as I would have liked to speak with him—in my prior encounters with Jason, in court, he seemed reasonable and relatively low key—I couldn't. I explained my ethical constraints. "You don't have to talk. Can't you just say 'uh huh' if you agree with what I'm saying or 'huh-uh' if you don't?" he asked. Funny guy. He continued to talk. He wanted to work this out. He didn't want to fight. I was itching to attempt to mediate a solution, but I couldn't. I asked him to give the phone back to Gerri. I let Gerri know my ideas about possible ways they could share the house. I also told her something that she and I already knew well: In order to work out this issue and all the other ones they'd face down the road in their divorce, the best thing Jason could do was hire new counsel.

SOME FAMILY LAWYERS relish a fight. They take on the causes of their clients with rabid abandon—the client's fight becomes the lawyer's personal crusade. And sometimes, as in this case, the lawyer amplifies the client's cause, raising the level of conflict rather than attempting to lower it.

This is clearly not how good family law practitioners should act. Our job is not to be cheerleaders for our clients. Our job is to be the cooler heads that prevail. We should calm, soothe, and problem-solve. We should care and be empathetic, sure, but we need a degree of dispassion to be effective. Even in the courtroom, that most adversarial of contexts, where our role is narrowed to one of pure advocacy for our client's position, it best serves both our profession and the people paying our bills to be dignified and professional and avoid mixing ourselves up with our clients.

Most lawyers get this. But some emphatically don't, and that's what gives divorce lawyers a bad name. It's also just so incredibly icky. It makes me embarrassed to be part of a system that generates such bitchiness and venom. One lawyer (who later ran unsuccessfully for a seat on the bench with the startling campaign slogan of "Never Been Sued for Malpractice") screamed at my stay-at-home-mom client in the hallway outside the courtroom after we left a child support hearing, "Get a job!" Another charming character also ran for judge and lost, thank God. This guy was so angry that I had tipped off the sheriffs that his client, who had an open arrest warrant for assaulting my client, was in the courthouse (thus resulting in my client having the incredibly satisfying experience of seeing her abusive ex taken away in handcuffs) that he got all red in the face and sputtered "You can suck my dick!" as I passed him in the hallway outside the courtroom. That, I have never forgotten. A new low in lawyer-to-lawyer relations.

These examples are absolutely the exception, though, rather than the rule. For the most part, my fellow members of the family-law bar get along famously. And it makes sense that we would. We're joined together through a common work life that can be difficult, emotionally intense, sometimes exhilarating, and sometimes thankless. We face one another as opponents again and again. Our clients come and go, but our relationships with one another can endure for decades.

Some clients find this shared history confusing and upsetting. They don't understand how I can zealously advocate for them against someone with whom I have a long-standing professional friendship. They assume that it will compromise their representation. They assume that I need to dislike opposing counsel as much as they dislike their exes. How, they ask, can I expect you to have my back in the courtroom, when I see you chatting with opposing counsel about where her oldest was accepted to college or where she's going on her next vacation?

Easy. Court is, at its most basic level, theater. There's a reason we put the judge in a black robe and the lawyers in suits (costumes) and have the lawyers stand in assigned places, rise to address the judge, and follow specific, formal protocols (stage directions). We are playing roles. Which does not mean we're playing games. Or that we don't care deeply about our clients and the outcome of their cases. These are serious and important components of a system that has evolved over centuries as an organized and effective way to resolve disputes. But they are roles, nonetheless, and when we leave the courtroom, we shed the role. Or we should. (Notable exception: see above, re: Mr. You-Can-Suck-My-Dick.)

I find that I can do my job better when I face a lawyer I know, trust, and respect and who presumably feels the same way about me. I have credibility with that lawyer, so when I forcefully explain why I expect to do better in court than what she's offering me to settle, she's likely to pay attention. When that lawyer outlines his position to me on a point of law we disagree about, I can imagine how he would argue the issue to a judge, how effective he'll be when he does it, and then take that into account in doing the delicate calculation about which to recommend to my client, settlement or trial. The benefit to my client is that the case is more likely to settle, and to settle better. That translates to lower legal fees and less emotional toll.

I WAS SITTING in the waiting room in motions court the other day with the dozen or so lawyers in the room, some of them chatting with one another, some joking with court staff, some with heads bent toward their clients, intently engaged in whispered conversation. Ghosts of cases past floated by as I gazed around me. There's James, elegant in a pinstripe suit and highly polished shoes, leaning against the wall and talking to a court officer about the Phillies. The officer, who has in front of him a list of the day's cases, is simultaneously checking in litigants and lawyers as they come into the waiting room and reading restaurant menus on his phone. I hear James call him "Squirrely"—apparently a courthouse nickname I was unaware of—and I feel a momentary tinge of jealousy. I wish I had that inside knowledge.

I haven't seen James for a long time. He doesn't primarily practice family law and I've had just one case with him, but I won't forget it; it's the only time I went to a prison to take the deposition of an inmate. My associate and I represented a woman whose boyfriend beat her to a pulp one night and left her unconscious on her living room floor. When she woke up and dragged herself to a hospital, it turned out she had a severe concussion, a broken nose, jaw, and cheekbone, and a ruptured eardrum. She ended up having multiple surgeries and being out of work for a year. Her boyfriend was convicted of the assault and went to prison. We filed a civil suit against him, seeking money damages to compensate her for her injuries, and James represented him in the civil suit. It seemed worth it to file because the guy had some real estate and money in the bank. He also had an MBA and at the time of the assault held a high-level corporate job, so the thought was that when he was released from prison he would eventually go back to making real money.

I wanted to depose the boyfriend to find out details about his assets and future employment prospects. Unlike in Stefan's wrongful death suit, where we wanted a big judgment as a matter of principle but had little expectation of ever seeing a dime, this case was all about our ability to collect. Procedurally, though, the cases were the same. Because of the boyfriend's conviction, we were able to jump over the hurdle of liability and move right to the question of how much money he should pay my client to compensate her for her injuries, both physical and psychological.

I don't generally go to prisons. In fact, the only other time I had been inside one was during a class in law school. This deposition was odd. The boyfriend wore a green prison jumpsuit and we sat at a rickety table, lawyers, defendant, and prison security. My client did not come. I had the impression that it was the highlight of the boyfriend's undoubtedly boring week, because it afforded him the opportunity to talk about all the money he had made, all the property he had acquired, what a great career he had, and how it had all been destroyed by my greedy client. He seemed to have no understanding whatsoever that he was responsible for almost killing her. Total disconnect. James sat next to his client, expressionless, and said little throughout. Later on in the case, James filed a motion to withdraw as counsel, I think because he wasn't being paid. We ended up receiving a large verdict. My client has not yet been able to collect any of it, but we remain hopeful that she may in the future.

Now James sees me looking at him, smiles, and goes back to joking with Squirrely.

Marianne is in the waiting room as well. She's short and squat. I'm tall and thin. Every time we stand side by side at counsel tables arguing a case, I think we must look like Mutt and Jeff. I'm remembering the first case I had against her. It was a divorce in which the major point of contention was that my client had received a large inheritance from her grandmother that she had deposited into a jointly titled account just two months before her husband announced that he wanted a divorce. Technically, the inheritance was marital property, since my client had not kept it separate, and Marianne's client was entitled to share it. But basic principles of fairness dictated otherwise, or so I argued. We reached a compromise on that one, after lots of push and pull.

As I look around the room, I see that Marianne is talking to Robert. It appears that they are opposing counsel in the case that is to be called into the courtroom next, according to Squirrely, who has now apparently selected a restaurant. Robert is a large, gentle, soft-spoken man. He wears rumpled suits and carries a battered briefcase and is crushingly effective at cross examination. Robert is always in the courthouse. He must not settle many cases or do much paperwork, because he seems to live at family court; at least, he's always there when I am. He's so nice but he currently represents a woman I cannot stand in a custody case I am handling, one that apparently will never, ever go away. (Despite my pledge not to become emotionally identified with my clients, this case is an exception; my client's ex-wife just gets under my skin. She has recently taken to emailing me—of course, I can't respond—and telling me, "as one mother to another," that I should be ashamed of myself.) Marianne, Bob, and their clients enter the courtroom, and the door shuts slowly behind them. Even though I know nothing about their case, I can picture how each of them will present it to the judge. I imagine Marianne talking fast and high, an urgent edge to her voice, and I know Robert will respond softly, slowing down the pace and the pitch, projecting calm and reason.

EARLIER THIS WEEK I had lunch with a lawyer I'd met only over the phone. We have a case together (meaning, we are opposing counsel) that we are diligently trying to settle. Notable elements involve boarding expenses for an elderly but much beloved horse and an incomprehensible prenuptial agreement entered into in the state of Oregon. I blog frequently about family law issues, and it turns out that Mark reads my posts and is interested in writing, himself, so he invited me to lunch. A couple of days before our date, I received a long letter from him outlining his client's response to our most recent settlement proposal. I had sent it to my client, who was not in the least inclined to accept it, which he told me in no uncertain terms. In fact, he commented that if he agreed to his wife's counterproposal, the horse would have it far better than he would.

Mark and I had a great time at lunch and discovered we had lots in common, including that both of us are celebrating thirtieth wedding anniversaries in the upcoming year (evidence supporting my theory that divorce lawyers are actually hopeless romantics; more on that later), and we both have children who are actors. We chatted about blogging, about some notorious criminal cases he had handled that he'd like to write about, and traded war stories from the family court trenches. We never mentioned his recent letter. After a pleasant hour, as I stood up to go back to my office, he said, "You know, we have to settle that case."

I nodded and said, "We will." And we will.

ANATOMY OF A TRIAL, PART IV:
Jessica/Credibility

One fifteen, back in Judge Diamond's courtroom. During the lunch break, Beth and I saw Brian's sister, Jessica, in the hallway, and I learned from Francis that he was going to call her to testify, "briefly." As Judge Diamond did not require that we exchange witness lists before trial, neither of us had an obligation to provide the other with advance notice of our witnesses. However, professional courtesy between counsel generally dictates otherwise, and Francis and I had actually discussed the topic. I told him about Marla, and he told me he wasn't sure if he was calling anyone other than his client, but he'd let me know. Which he didn't. So Jessica was a surprise.

Francis rises. "Your Honor, we call Jessica Foster." The judge looks over at his crier (essentially, the maître-d' of the courtroom), who stands up, leaves the room, and returns a moment later with Brian's younger sister. Jessica appears to be about thirty; slim, blond, pretty, fashionably dressed.

The crier leads her to the witness stand and tells her to place her left hand on the Bible and raise her right hand.

"Do you swear that the testimony you are about to give will be the truth, the whole truth, and nothing but the truth, so help you God?"

"I do."

"You may be seated."

Jessica takes her left hand off the Bible, lowers her right hand, smoothes the back of her skirt, and sits down.

Judge Diamond looks at Francis, who's standing at counsel table, notes in hand. "Counsel, your witness."

This exchange takes place every day, multiple times, in every courtroom in the country. It's so routine that it can seem almost inconsequential, just another item to check off before the witness starts to talk, like the judge making sure he has the case file with him on the bench, or the court reporter putting a roll of paper in her stenotype machine. But the gravity of the oath is tremendous. It's the backbone of our legal system. It's our chosen method of determining whether someone is telling the truth. The presumption is that if a witness is under oath, she is doing so. Unless she gives the judge or jury a reason to think she's not—through her demeanor, internal contradictions in her testimony, or external contradictions from other evidence admitted in the case—her sworn testimony will be assumed to be true.

Still, often it's not. People lie under oath. Frequently.

This may sound obvious—of course they do, otherwise we wouldn't need trials to determine "the truth"—but it's actually quite shocking when it happens right in front of you. When a witness lies, my clients tend to gasp, shake their heads, or sometimes even cry out (always to be admonished by the judge to be quiet, you'll have/you've had your turn to speak, now it's his/her turn). And, actually, "lying" is a complicated concept. Often people have different memories of the same event. During the course of a trial, the testimony sometimes comes in like a Venn diagram, with witnesses' narratives arranging themselves in overlapping spheres, leaving the judge with one central agreed-upon fact and the rest of the versions radiating outward from that center, sometimes in radically different directions.

In custody cases, the people most commonly called as witnesses are family members. Grandparents, aunts, uncles, and other relatives are usually the people best situated to describe the day-to-day details of how parents care for their children and how children relate to their parents. They have the knowledge the court wants. Unfortunately, they are notoriously unreliable witnesses. Blood is definitely thicker than water. If you expect a mother to acknowledge her son's explosive temper—even when she and his wife witnessed a particular outburst at the same Thanksgiving dinner—you are generally fooling yourself. She will either lie outright or significantly downplay his conduct. If what's at stake is her son's losing custodial time with her grandchildren, she is highly unlikely, in my experience, to back up her daughter-in-law's version of events.

I have no reason to think Jessica will be an exception to this rule. After we learned during the lunch break that she would be testifying, I had Beth give me a crash course on everything Jessica knows that could be relevant to custody. Beth has spent a lot of time with Jessica. She told me she thought of her as a little sister and that Jessica confided in her, including confidences about Brian. Jessica told her about fights Brian used to get in during high school, about the classmate whose nose Brian broke, and about how their father had such a hard time controlling Brian during that period that they once got into a fist fight as well. One time when Jessica was visiting them, Brian became angry and yelled at Beth because he couldn't find his car keys, calling her a "stupid bitch" in front of Jessica, Jimmy, and Kaitlyn. Beth specifically remembers that, right after this outburst, Jessica pulled her into the kitchen and told her Brian had always been "that way," and that he used to criticize Jessica's clothing and tell her she looked like a slut. "Be careful, because he's crazy," Beth remembers Jessica saying as she left their house that afternoon. When we saw her in the hallway this afternoon, Beth was shocked. Given what Jessica knows about him, why would Brian want to call her?

In order to prepare for my cross-examination, I asked Beth for any information she had about Brian and Jessica's current relationship. Beth thought they had become closer since the separation, as the children often mentioned seeing Jessica when they returned from weekends with their father. And she knew that a couple of months before she and Brian separated, Jessica lost her job and fell behind on her student loan payments and Brian stepped in and made them for her. "But that wouldn't cause her to lie," Beth said. "I can't believe he's calling her as a witness. She'll be under oath. She'll have to testify about what she saw that day, and about what she said to me, right?"

"We'll see," I said.

Francis takes Jessica through the preliminaries: where she lives (same neighborhood as Brian); what her relationship is to Brian (younger sister); what she does for a living (restaurant manager, laid off seven months ago, looking for work).

"Do you have occasion to spend time with your brother and his children?"

"Yes."

"How often?"

"Do you mean before or after he had to move out of his house?"

"Let's start with before."

"Okay, so I used to visit him and Beth and the kids sometimes, maybe once every couple of months, and we'd always see each other at family functions or whenever our mother was in town. And sometimes I would babysit for Kaitlyn and Jimmy."

"And since the separation?"

"I've been seeing my brother a lot since he had to move into the apartment. I helped him decorate it, and I usually stop by on the weekends he has the kids, just to visit. And if he's taking them someplace, he'll call and ask me if I want to come. Like a few weeks ago, I went with him and the kids to the Franklin Institute. They had a blast."

I can hear a muffled choking sound coming from my left side, where Beth is sitting. The Franklin Institute is Philadelphia's science museum. "He's never taken them to a museum in his life," whispered Beth. "His lawyer must've told him to take them there." I shush her and give her a piece of paper to write down comments so I can read them before I start my cross.

"How would you describe your brother as a parent?"

"He's an awesome dad. He lives for those kids. He plays sports with them, he takes them camping, he takes them fishing, they play cards, he just has lots of fun with them. It's really hard on him now that he only gets to see them every other weekend."

This is a tough call. I could object to the "it's really hard on him" statement and ask the judge to strike it, because it's not responsive to the question and it's outside the witness's knowledge. She cannot testify to Brian's state of mind. But if I move to strike it from the record, which in all likelihood Judge Diamond will do, I'm giving Francis the opportunity to lay the appropriate foundation to get that testimony admitted, and it will be much stronger. He'll ask her to describe how her brother acts when the kids leave after the weekend, or he'll ask what changes, if any, she has observed in her brother since the separation, and this will give Jessica the opportunity to go way deeper into this issue. She could end up describing Brian crying when the kids leave or having lost weight or being unable to sleep, or something much more damaging than the off-the-cuff "it's really hard on him." On balance, I decide it's not worth pursuing and I let it pass.

"Have you ever had occasion to see your brother discipline the children?"

"Well, not really. I mean he talks to them if they do something wrong, just talks to them and corrects them, you know, that's all. And sometimes he makes them go to their rooms for a time-out."

"Have you ever seen your brother physically discipline either of the children?"

"Oh no, never anything physical. And really, it just doesn't come up very often because they're so good around him. My niece is a total daddy's girl and Jimmy just hangs on his dad's every word."

Beth is writing furiously. I am wondering whether Francis is going to ask Jessica anything about Beth and, if so, if Jessica will say anything negative. Since Brian is seeking equally shared, rather than primary, physical custody, it wouldn't be logical to trash Beth's parenting; if you want to share custody, you have to be willing to acknowledge that the other parent does a good job. However, since Beth has accused Brian of abusing Jimmy, it would help his case if Jessica could provide some support for the theme of his defense, the theory that Beth has manufactured the whole accusation because she wants to punish Brian for having an affair.

"No further questions."

That answers it. Francis has decided to limit Jessica's direct testimony to the topic of "Brian is a great parent." He's going to let anything negative she has to say about Beth come out, if at all, in response to my cross, where she won't have a choice, where it will seem to be reluctantly pulled out of her. He is calculating that she will appear more believable that way, more neutral. I consider waiving any cross of Jessica, as Judge Diamond knows that family members will sing the praises of their relatives in custody cases, and therefore he's likely to take Jessica's testimony with a grain of salt. But I don't want to let the student loan issue go unmentioned, as that fact provides a specific, concrete motive for her to lie for Brian, in addition to the generic bias that can be implied just because she's his sister.

Judge Diamond looks at me. "Cross-examination."

I decide to cross and to go right for that issue.

"Ms. Foster, you love your brother, don't you?"

"Of course."

"And you wouldn't want anything bad to happen to him, would you?"

I can see it dawning on her where I'm going. She sits up straighter and stops smiling.

"Of course I wouldn't, but I wouldn't lie for him."

"You testified in response to questions from Mr. DiLorenzo that you lost your job seven months ago, right?"

"Yes."

"Did you go to college?"

"Objection." Francis stands up. "Relevance and outside the scope of direct."

"Counsel?"

"Your Honor, I'm laying the foundation for a line of questioning that goes to the witness's credibility." Questions that shed light on bias, on motive to lie, on general credibility — in short, on whether a witness is likely to be telling the truth or not — are, with certain narrow exceptions, permissible, even if the subject matter wouldn't otherwise be relevant. Even though on cross-examination counsel is generally limited to the topics covered during the witness's direct testimony, that rule is applied loosely to questions that go to the issue of credibility.

Francis responds, before being asked to by the judge, "What possible relevance does whether this witness went to college have to her credibility? Is counsel trying to insinuate that someone without a college education is more likely to lie?"

Clearly, Francis is unaware of the student loan issue.

"Your Honor, that's ridiculous. Of course not. If the

court permits me to pursue this line of questioning, it'll be clear what the relevance is to the witness's credibility."

"All right, counsel. Objection overruled. Mr. DiLorenzo, this is cross-examination, so I'm giving Ms. Klaw some leeway here. Continue."

Jessica looks confused. Judge Diamond turns back toward the witness stand. "You may answer the question, Ms. Foster."

"Okay. Yes, I went to college. I have a B.A. from St. Joe's."

"Did you take out student loans?"

"Objection!" Francis jumps to his feet.

"Overruled." Judge Diamond doesn't even wait for me to respond.

"After you lost your job, you had difficulty making your student loan payments, didn't you?"

Jessica looks quizzical. She is not understanding why I'm asking her this and she's trying to figure it out.

"Yes, it was hard, I mean I was getting unemployment, but with my rent and stuff . . ."

"So you asked your brother, Mr. Foster, if he could help you out, didn't you?"

"Yes. I didn't have anyone else to help me."

She just figured out the reason for these questions. She shoots Beth a poisonous look.

"And he did help you out, right?"

"Yes, he did. Because he's a great guy."

"He's a great guy and he's done you a big favor, right?"

"Well, yes, but I'm going to pay him back."

"When you get a job?"

"Yes, when I get a job."

"But right now you're still unemployed, correct?"

"Yes."

"So Brian—Mr. Foster—is continuing to make your loan payments for you, isn't he?"

"Yes."

"And when you testified on direct examination, you didn't tell the court any bad things about your brother, did you?"

"No."

"In fact you said," I look down at my notes, "that he was an 'awesome parent,' right?"

"Yes, he is."

"Was he being an awesome parent when he screamed at my client in front of you and both children and called her a 'stupid bitch'?"

"He never did that."

"So if my client testifies about this incident, which took place at her house when Mr. Foster couldn't find his car keys, she'd be lying?"

"Yes. I don't remember anything like that."

"Does that mean you also don't remember telling her that day to be careful, because your brother is crazy?"

"No! I never said that."

"Would you agree with me that if your brother called my client a stupid bitch in front of Kaitlyn and Jimmy, that would not be consistent with being an 'awesome dad'?"

Francis scrambles to his feet. "Objection. The witness testified that she does not recall any such incident. The question is improper. And argumentative."

"Counsel." Stern look from Judge Diamond. "I agree with Mr. DiLorenzo. Can you rephrase?"

I don't need to rephrase. I've made my point, for whatever it's worth. I hope I've now planted a second seed in the judge's mind that Brian has a dark side and, hopefully, tempered Jessica's glowing account of her brother's parenting by pointing out her indebtedness to him.

"I'll withdraw the question, Your Honor. And I have no further questions for Ms. Foster."

Judge Diamond asks Francis if he has any questions on redirect. Predictably, even though she already said it during cross, he does. He'll want to make it clear that her brother's helping her with the loans is not a reason for her to lie.

"When your brother agreed to help you with your student loans, did he ask for anything in return?"

"Well, I told him I would pay him back when I found a job, and he agreed."

"Anything else?"

"No."

"Did you and he discuss what your testimony would be today?"

"No."

I know, as sure as the sun will rise tomorrow, that this cannot be true. Every family I've ever worked with discusses and dissects everything going on in a custody case. It's just not humanly possible that they didn't talk about her testimony. But she's never going to admit it and I'm not going to give her the chance to say it twice. I don't plan on doing any recross unless I hear something I'm not expecting.

"And you know you're under oath today?"

"Yes."

"No further questions."

I decline recross.

"Ms. Foster, you are excused. Mr. DiLorenzo, who's your next witness?"

"Mr. Foster, Your Honor."

"Okay. We'll take a ten-minute break and begin with Father's testimony when we return."

Beth is whispering to me as we walk out into the hallway. She's speaking really fast and she's clearly upset by Jessica's testimony. "How come you didn't ask her about Brian getting into fights in high school and about the fight with their dad?" Even though a parent's violent conduct is considered relevant in a custody case in my jurisdiction, there are parameters. Based on the fact that Judge Diamond limited Beth's testimony about Brian's abusive conduct toward her in the recent past, I am positive that evidence about fights between Brian and his teenage peers over twenty years ago is way too remote, both in time and in substance. If Brian had abused a child when he was a teenager, I might be able to get evidence of that admitted. If he'd broken someone's nose a year ago, I would expect the judge to want to hear about it. Trying to introduce evidence about Brian's high school brawls, though, would make Beth and me look like we were grasping at straws, like this was all we had. Also, given that she denied that the "stupid bitch" incident ever took place, it's highly unlikely that Jessica would have admitted to telling Beth about Brian's out-of-control teenage years.

Whispering outside the courtroom so Brian and his lawyer won't hear, I attempt to convey a condensed version of my thinking to Beth. There's a certain amount of self-preservation going on in a conversation like this. While it's good for Beth to understand the reasoning behind my decision not to ask Jessica the teenage-fight questions, what I really want her to know is that this was a strategic decision, not the result of my forgetting important information she told me. Because that does sometimes happen, and it's embarrassing. In an instance like this, where it didn't, it could still seem to Beth as though I'm just trying to justify, after the fact, a memory lapse in the courtroom.

Now Beth is focused on Jessica's denial of the "stupid bitch" incident. She is shaking her head in disbelief, telling me again how she thought of Jessica as a sister. I am only half listening. I'm too busy assessing the impact of Jessica's testimony. Overall, quite helpful to Brian. Jessica seemed forthright, she looked directly at Judge Diamond when she testified, and she didn't become overly defensive during my cross. Although the student loan issue was certainly worth raising, whatever effect it may have had was far from a bombshell. I could put Beth back on the stand for rebuttal to testify about the "stupid bitch" incident, both as to what Brian said (because he's the opposing party) and what she observed (that the kids were present and how it affected them). But the fact that I didn't question her about it during her direct exam, that she would only be testifying to it after Jessica has denied it, would weaken the impact of the testimony. And Jessica's statements to Beth about the teenage fights are not going to be admissible under any circumstances.

Beth is still shaking her head about her sister-in-law's dishonesty. I glance at my phone; the ten minutes is almost up. We need to go back into the courtroom.

ANATOMY OF A TRIAL PART V:
Brian/Cross Examination

Judge Diamond has already retaken the bench. Getting a nod from the court reporter that she's ready to go, he turns toward Francis.

"Counsel, we're running short on time here. It's two thirty and I need to finish at five. I will not be keeping my staff late. Ms. Monroe here has to pick up her daughter from day care at five thirty and I got in big trouble for making her late once already this week. Right, Ms. Monroe?"

The judge's clerk, who's sitting across from the court reporter in front of a computer and a two-foot-high pile of files, smiles at her boss. "Right, Your Honor. They charge me a dollar a minute for being late."

"So, counsel," says the judge, turning back to Francis and me, "you can see I have no choice here. If Ms. Monroe isn't happy I can't run this courtroom. So we are finishing at five p.m. sharp. I will want to interview both children, separately. I expect those interviews to be brief, so I'll start them at four. Mr. DiLorenzo, in addition to your client, do you have any other witnesses?"

"I have the Child Protective Services worker, Your Honor."

"Can counsel stipulate?"

This is good for us. I'm happy to stipulate (to put an agreement on the record in lieu of having Ms. Williams testify) that the report of suspected child abuse was unfounded. The significance of a finding of unfounded by CPS is very limited in scope, and Judge Diamond will know that. It just means that the caseworker could not independently corroborate the report of suspected child abuse made by Marla Peres. We all know exactly what happened: Beth told her what Jimmy said, Brian denied it, Kaitlyn didn't know anything about it, and Jimmy wouldn't talk. So she closed her case. It doesn't mean we can't successfully prove that Brian caused the bruise in the far more nuanced setting of the courtroom. And if the caseworker doesn't testify, if we just stipulate to her conclusion and move on, that eliminates the risk of her saying something damaging about Beth (for instance, "Ms. Foster was really upset she couldn't be in the room with me when I interviewed Jimmy") or something positive about Brian ("Mr. Foster was so cooperative"). Francis, of course, would prefer to put Ms. Williams on the stand, for the same reasons I would like to exclude her, but he's in a bind.

If Ms. Williams testifies, even if Francis conducts a very brief direct exam, I can run the clock by stretching out my cross. Francis and I both know that the judge's schedule is extremely tight; he's booked months in advance. And as long as the trial isn't finished, the status quo will continue and the temporary order limiting Brian's custodial time to alternate weekends and Wednesdays will stay in effect. Is it worth it? Francis is apparently deciding that whatever benefit he can get out of the CPS worker is outweighed by taking time away from Brian or possibly prolonging the trial.

"We're willing to stipulate that the CPS report was unfounded, Your Honor, and we would ask for the admission of the letter from CPS to that effect dated February twenty eighth of this year." I agree, quickly.

"Very good. The letter from CPS will be admitted as Father's Exhibit 1. Are you now calling Mr. Foster? Remember, we have to be done by 4." Turning to his crier, Judge Diamond directs him to go out to the hallway and tell "the lady from CPS" that he will not be needing her and she is excused.

BRIAN WALKS UP to the witness stand and sits down. He's wearing a white shirt and a red tie. He appears calm and confident. Francis covers necessary and uncontroversial ground, establishing where Brian lives, introducing into evidence photos of his apartment, which show that he has a bedroom for each child, appropriately outfitted. Kaitlyn's is lavender ("she picked the color") and Jimmy's is stacked high with Legos ("they're his favorite"). Francis has Brian explain that he is permitted to use the backyard as part of his lease, and introduces pictures of a fenced and manicured yard, complete with swing set and wading pool. Then he questions Brian about his job (Brian's a pharmacist, which makes him sound both smart and responsible) and his schedule (he has seniority at the drugstore where he works, so he can choose shifts that are compatible with an equally shared custody schedule; he can load his required number of shifts into days the kids are with Beth and work less when they are with him).

Francis is moving along at a fast pace and there's nothing objectionable about the questions. The judge is writing on his pad while Brian talks, perhaps notes about Brian's testimony, perhaps something entirely different. A draft of a letter in some other case? A to-do list? I have no way of knowing. What I do know is that Francis is setting up the external requirements, including suitable accommodations and availability, for Brian to have shared custody, and we won't be disputing this evidence, so I might as well let it come in quickly.

Francis moves to the what-kind-of-parent-are-you line of questioning. I perk up.

"What kinds of activities do you like to do with your children?"

"Well, I love the outdoors, and so do they. Since Jimmy was a baby, I've taken them camping, and during the last year or so we've started going fishing. We go down the shore to my brother's place and go out on his boat with him and his kids, their cousins. Kait and Jimmy love it down there."

"Anything else?"

"I'm also big on educational activities. Like I took them into the city to the Franklin Institute, where they had an exhibit on robots. And then there's just the normal stuff like playing catch and things like that. And I'm going to put Jimmy in Cub Scouts this year. I plan to be a troop leader."

"Brian, how do you discipline Jimmy and Kaitlyn?"

Francis is warming up the crowd by calling his client by his first name. He's trying to send a signal that Brian is just like you and me, just a regular guy, but it's misplaced. There is no crowd and no jury to play to, and Judge Diamond won't care what name he uses.

"I don't need to. They're such good kids."

Ms. Monroe, the clerk whose child has to be picked up from day care at 5:30 sharp, shifts in her chair and looks skeptically at Brian. The bubble over her head reads: Really? Never?

"Do you ever use corporal punishment?"

"Absolutely not. I would never hit my children. I don't believe in that."

"Now, Brian, you heard your wife testify earlier about an incident where you tied your son to a chair and allegedly made him eat some chicken; do you remember that?"

"Yes."

"Did you do that?"

"Well, I remember the incident, but it wasn't at all the way she described it. We had a booster seat that you had to attach to the chair, and the strap broke and fell off it. I didn't want to put Jimmy in the seat without it being strapped to the chair, because he moves around so much I was afraid the seat would just fall off the chair and he would hit his head on the floor or something. So I used a belt to go under the chair and over his lap in the seat, you know, to, like, secure him and the booster seat in the chair. It was a safety thing. And Beth was right there; she didn't say anything about it."

"And did you force him to eat?"

"No, not at all. We had a rule that the kids had to try everything on their plates, and Jimmy was being really stubborn and saying he hated chicken and didn't want to taste it. So I told him he had to stay at the table until he did."

"Did you force food into his mouth?"

"No, of course not."

"Brian, you've also heard Ms. Foster's testimony about a bruise on your son's arm. Did you cause that bruise?"

"No."

"Do you know how he got it?"

"I really have no idea. Maybe at school during tumbling class or just playing at home. He's into everything. He gets lots of bumps and scrapes. He's just a normal little boy. It's just not a big deal."

Bad phrase. First stumble. I write it down.

"So you've testified you never force-fed your son, right?"

"Yes."

"And you've testified you didn't intentionally bruise Jimmy's arm, right?"

"Yes."

"Do you have any idea why your wife would accuse you of these things?"

"Objection. Calls for speculation."

Judge Diamond looks at Francis. "Counsel? Ms. Klaw is correct. Where are you going with this?"

"I'll rephrase, your Honor. Mr. Foster, did you have any conversations with your wife that relate to these accusations?"

"Yes."

"What were they?"

"Well, I did something very wrong. Our marriage has been on the rocks for a long time, and — "

Here it comes. I stand up quickly, wanting to cut this off. "Move to strike. Nonresponsive. The question was whether he had any conversations with my client."

Francis makes a face. "Your Honor, she interrupted my client. He was simply giving background information relating to a conversation he had with his wife, which is directly relevant to the veracity of her statements. And responsive to my question."

"All right, Mr. DiLorenzo, I won't strike the testimony, but get to the point. Move this along."

"You were saying, Mr. Foster?"

"I was saying that our marriage had been very bad for a long time, and I did something I'm not proud of. I had an affair. And Beth found out about it, and she went ballistic. She yelled and screamed and threw me out of the house and told me she would make sure I never saw my kids again."

Good, I think. If she did say anything like this, it's clearly hyperbole, said in the heat of the moment. He's not claiming she made a specific threat to accuse him of abuse. And maybe it's so far from being a specific threat about the allegations at issue here that it's not even relevant. I jump up, a delayed reaction. "Objection. Move to strike. This is not testimony about a conversation relating to the specific allegations counsel asked Mr. Foster about, force-feeding Jimmy and bruising his arm. The witness is recounting a marital argument, and given that these people are getting divorced, I'm sure my client could testify about many such arguments, but it has nothing to do with the allegations that the witness was asked about." Not sure this makes sense, but worth a try.

"Counsel," says the judge to me, looking a bit exasperated, "I wasn't born yesterday. I will take this testimony for what it is and give it the appropriate weight. Motion denied."

Which means he won't pay much attention to it. Good.

"Anything further, Mr. DiLorenzo? We still have cross

examination and my interviews of the children. I'm not going to tell you how to try your case, but I think I've got the idea."

Francis takes the instruction. "Briefly, Mr. Foster, you also heard your wife testify about some marital disputes, which she contends got physical. Do you remember that?

"Yes."

"Brian, did you ever pinch or slap your wife, as she has alleged?"

"Never. She sometimes would hit me, though."

Beth opens her mouth in astonishment, as though to say something. I instinctively put my hand on her arm and she catches her breath.

"And do you also recall your wife's testimony about some plates you allegedly broke?"

"Yes."

"Did you break those plates?"

"I'm not going to lie. We did have an argument where a couple of plates were broken, but Beth started the fight, and she broke the first plate."

"Brian, did you ever physically abuse your wife in any way?"

"Never."

"Do you have any idea why your wife would accuse you of physically abusing her?"

I jump up. "Objection! Your Honor, this has already

been ruled on. Calls for speculation, just like the last time counsel asked this question."

"Sustained," said the judge without even looking up. But Francis made his point. He knew the question was improper and that his client wouldn't be allowed to answer it, but it served a purpose; it reminded the judge of the earlier testimony about Beth allegedly saying that Brian would never see his kids again, so that maybe, when he's mulling over the evidence, Judge Diamond will decide that Beth's accusations were either made up entirely or exaggerated.

"No further questions, Your Honor."

"Cross-examination. Ms. Klaw, it is now three thirty and we are stopping at four for the children's interviews. Right, Ms. Monroe?"

"Right, Your Honor." The affable Ms. Monroe was clearly used to this particular courtroom shtick. She is Judge Diamond's foil, his excuse for shutting down at 5:00.

CROSS-EXAMINATION OF BRIAN is a delicate matter. I'm not going to get him to admit he slapped or pinched Beth, or stuffed chicken in Jimmy's mouth, or punished him by squeezing his arm so hard that it caused the large and startling bruise. If I were to ask him directly about those accusations, it would just give him the opportunity to reinforce the testimony he gave on direct, to deny it all again, perhaps more eloquently and confidently this time; perhaps he would add something new that he forgot to say in response to his own lawyer's questioning. My goal is a more subtle one. I want to nip around the edges of his testimony to show inconsistencies and to highlight anything improbable. And while doing so, I hope to make him angry without overtly badgering him. I want him to fly off the handle, to be rude to me, to show exasperation. I want the judge to see that this guy really has a hair trigger, that this is a father who cannot control himself even in the middle of his custody trial. I want to show that the persona Brian presented during his direct testimony was just a smooth, scripted, well-rehearsed façade.

I never know where I'm going to start on cross-examination. I have a list of topics and questions I make in preparation for trial, and then another list I scribble down as the witness is testifying on direct. I have all those notes in front of me and I just dive in. I don't have a road map when I start. I feel my way through, touching down here, touching down there, seeing what works, abandoning what doesn't. It's a very creative part of trial work. I love it.

"Mr. Foster, you just testified that you never needed to discipline your children because they're such good kids, isn't that correct?"

"Yes."

"Meaning you have never, in the eight years since Kaitlyn was born, had to correct any behavior of either of your children?"

"Not really."

I'm not really sure where I'm going with this, but my instinct is it's a good area to push him on, because it's so unbelievable.

"Are your children afraid of you, Mr. Foster?"

"Of course not."

Brian is starting to scowl at me.

"When Jimmy wouldn't eat the chicken, wasn't keeping him in his chair a form of discipline?"

"I guess so."

"And wasn't forcing him to eat it a punishment for breaking one of your rules?"

"I didn't say I forced him to eat it."

"Well, you testified that you made him sit at the table until he did, right?"

"Yes."

"And he didn't want to be at that table, did he?"

"No."

"And you had him tied to the chair with your belt, didn't you?"

"It wasn't like that. He was strapped into his seat."

"Mr. Foster, was your belt tied around Jimmy's lap?"

"Yes."

"And buckled tight so he was restrained?"

"Yes, because I wanted him to be safe."

"So you would agree with me, then, that he was being forced to sit at the table?"

"Well, restrained."

"Okay, restrained. In the sense that he was not free to leave, correct?"

"Yes."

"And he didn't want to eat his chicken, right?"

"Right."

"And it's your testimony that he just spontaneously decided to take a bite of it?"

"Well, after a while."

"He was crying, wasn't he?"

"I don't recall."

"Beth was really upset, wasn't she?"

"Not that I recall."

"You don't remember or she wasn't?"

Francis sees an opening. "Objection. Asked and answered. The witness said he didn't recall."

"Overruled. This is cross-examination. Continue, Ms. Klaw. But remember that I am going to cut you off at four p.m. I think you've made your point."

I'm not sure myself what point Judge Diamond thinks I've made. I'm really just playing with this, seeing where it leads.

"Mr. Foster, you can answer the question."

"I don't remember."

"So you don't remember whether Jimmy was crying and you don't remember whether your wife was upset but you do remember that you didn't force-feed him the chicken, is that right?"

"That's right."

I've milked this for all I can. I need to move on.

"So as you've said, Jimmy's a really good kid, isn't he?"

"Both my children are."

"So good that you've never had to discipline him, right?"

"Right."

"And he tells the truth, doesn't he?"

"Not always. He's only five."

"So sometimes he lies?"

"I don't know I would call it lying. Sometimes he tells stories."

"Sometimes he tells stories." I'm stalling for time. This is good; I know I can go somewhere with this.

"And he's just a little boy, right?"

"Yes."

"So the stories he tells would be stories about things he's familiar with, correct?"

"I don't know."

Answer doesn't matter.

"Your testimony is that when Jimmy wouldn't eat his chicken you made him stay in his booster seat until he did, isn't it?"

"Yes."

"And that's not really discipline, that's just you enforcing a house rule, right?"

"Yes."

"And you believe your children should learn to take responsibility for themselves, don't you?"

"Yes, I do."

"So if Jimmy, for example, spilled grape juice on a rug at your apartment, you'd want him to clean it up, wouldn't you?"

"Sure."

"And if he didn't, you'd be mad, wouldn't you?"

"No."

"Well, you were mad about him not eating the chicken, weren't you?"

"No."

"Did Jimmy spill grape juice on your carpet?"

"Yes."

"Did you make him clean it up?"

"I made him help me, yes."

"He didn't want to, did he?"

"Well, no, not really; he's only five."

"But you made him, didn't you?"

"Sure. Yes."

"Did you have to restrain him like you restrained him at the table?"

Brian's face is getting red.

"No."

I'm continuing to ignore the answers.

"So if you wanted him to clean the carpet and he wouldn't, you'd have to hold on to him to get him to do it, right?"

"Well, I didn't."

"Since he wasn't strapped in anywhere, you'd probably have to hold him by one of his arms, right?"

I can't believe Francis isn't objecting. He's letting me continue to ask questions about events that have not been testified to; these are questions of the "when did you stop beating your wife" variety. But I'm on a roll, so I keep going.

"And if he wanted to get away from you, you'd have to hold him really hard, wouldn't you?"

"Objection! This has gone far enough! Counsel is assuming facts not in evidence."

"Sustained. Ms. Klaw, that's enough."

"I'll withdraw the question, Your Honor."

I'm happy.

"Mr. Foster, you didn't tell my client about the spilled grape juice incident, did you?"

"No. There was nothing to tell and I don't expect her to tell me every time one of the kids spills something."

"But this was an incident that upset Jimmy, didn't it?"

Brian shrugged. "No, not really."

"Then why did you tell him not to tell his mother about it?"

"I didn't. Why would I do that?"

Judge Diamond looks over at Brian. "Mr. Foster, you cannot ask counsel questions. Your attorney will have an opportunity to re-direct you after cross examination."

"Jimmy loves you, doesn't he, Mr. Foster?"

"Yes, and I love him."

"And Jimmy wants to please you, right?"

"Sure."

"So he would do what you say, wouldn't he?"

"Well, sometimes. Like I keep saying, he just turned five—of course he doesn't always do what I say."

"But you never need to discipline him, right?"

"Right."

"And didn't you testify that's because he's so good he always does what he's told?"

"Yes."

"So if you told him to say something he'd say it, right?"

"I guess."

"And if you told him not to say something, he wouldn't say it, right?"

"No, that's not right because I wouldn't tell him not to say anything."

"But if you did, you expect that he would follow your instructions, right?"

"Objection. The question was asked and answered and now counsel is posing a hypothetical again."

"Sustained. Ms. Klaw, you need to wrap this up."

I think I've gotten all I can. Brian is sweating and his face is red. He looks like he's trying hard to contain himself. He looks—I hope—like someone who might force food into his child's mouth and squeeze his arm so hard that he bruises it.

"I'm done, Your Honor. No further questions."

"Redirect?"

Francis follows up with some questions about the grape juice incident and asks Brian if he ever asked either of the children to lie about anything. Brian answers with an emphatic no. The clock over Judge Diamond's head reads 4:05. The judge looks at me.

"No recross, right, Counsel?" This is not a question. It's an imperative.

"No, Your Honor."

"I thought not. Good. I'd like the parties to stay in the courtroom while I interview the children in chambers. Counsel, please follow me." The judge looks at his court officer. "Mr. Doyle, let's start with Jimmy. Give us a minute to get settled and then you can bring him in."

Stuff

Everyone knows that when a couple divorces, they have to divvy up assets they accumulated during their life together. Houses, cars, bank accounts, investments, and retirement benefits are all on the table to be shuffled and redistributed. To be sure, I spend a lot of time negotiating exactly how this should happen, but ultimately it all comes down to money, for example, how much is the house worth compared to the 401(k)?

Not so with stuff. Furniture, artwork (of the still-life-your-friend-painted-in-art-school variety, not the signed-Picasso-print variety), photographs, kitchen wares—in other words, the dreaded category of "personal property"—can be the bane of the divorce lawyer's existence. People with millions of dollars in investments can end up fighting over a piece of pottery someone picked up at a roadside market in Tulum. Dividing up stuff is not about money. It's about emotion. I try to avoid these negotiations like the plague. I generally tell clients "I don't do furniture," meaning, work it out yourselves, because it's a total waste of time and money to pay lawyers to argue about why one spouse should get the print of the lilies rather than the water color of the Cape Cod sunset. How are we supposed to know? And also, this is not why I went to law school.

But. I do understand that stories and history and family culture are embodied in the stuff we acquire as the years pass, and sometimes lawyers can't avoid being pulled into the mix. If that happens, and if I start to feel irritated about it, I have developed a sure-fire way to put at least a temporary damper on my grumpiness and summon forth the empathy necessary to get the job done. I go straight to an example of stuff acquired during my own marriage that I would lie down in front of a truck for: my Christmas decorations. I love them. I love acquiring a couple of beautiful new ornaments each year. I love the Play Doh, macaroni-and-glue Santas my kids made in preschool. I love the Popsicle-stick reindeer with the googly eyes they made in first grade (same art teacher, exact same holiday project three years later). I love the holiday candles and garlands I put on the mantel. Woe be to the man who wants to take those treasures from me! So I get it. Still, I'm much more comfortable thinking through what to do with my clients' stock options than their KitchenAid mixers.

Sometimes people use possessions as a weapon. I had a divorce case in which the settlement agreement provided for the parties to share their only child's bat mitzvah photographs as follows: the husband was to keep the album made by the photographer and the wife (my client) was to keep all the prints. Sounds reasonable, right? This is just the kind of solution to the problem-I-didn't-want-to-solve-in-the-first-place for which I pat myself on the back, thinking, Job well done! They were fighting over the photos; I figured it out, tied it all up in a bow, and would never have to hear about the issue again.

Unfortunately, in that case, not so. When the two hundred–plus prints were finally (and reluctantly) delivered to my client, she discovered that all the pictures that included her family members were missing. The husband adamantly denied that he had anything to do with this, we couldn't track down the photographer, and no one had the negatives (remember those?). In fact, the husband went so far as to blame my client, accusing her of removing all the pictures of her relatives years earlier after a fight she had with her sister. Infuriating. And my emotions were so mixed. I felt righteous anger on my client's behalf because I knew how important the photos were to her and because her husband was being such an absolute jerk. I was also annoyed with her (totally unfairly, I realize) because now I had to deal with this issue again. I was irritated that my solution hadn't worked. I felt ineffective. Those photos were gone and she was never going to see them again. And when I thought about it, we shouldn't have been surprised. This was the same man who, the night she left him, made a bonfire with her wedding dress in the backyard. Really, she was lucky just to get away and leave the stuff behind.

AND THEN THERE are pets. A devoted pet owner (or "pet parent," as my pet health insurance company so cozily refers to its customers) myself, I certainly don't think of them as "stuff"; legally, though, they generally are. At least, in Pennsylvania, pets are personal property. Your dog has the same status in your divorce as your coffee table. And—will this surprise you?—divorcing spouses sometimes disagree over who keeps the dog. Or the cat. Or the three cats, because they can't be separated! Sometimes the disagreement is of the "I want him"/ "no, I want him" variety, and sometimes it's the "you take him"/ "no, you take him" type. Some people agree to share the dog, meeting at a designated exchange location every couple of weeks. And sometimes the dog travels between the ex-spouses' households with the kids. But whatever the solution, divorcing couples have to figure it out themselves because there is no recourse in court. If the golden retriever—let's call her Goldie—belonged to the husband before they married, for example (thus making Goldie "nonmarital" property), the wife cannot ask a judge to order visitation so she can continue to see Goldie. You're on your own with the animals.

I was in court before the divorce master (a lawyer who works for the court whose job is to try to help people settle their cases) for what both parties and both attorneys assumed would produce a final settlement after two years of unsuccessful negotiation. My client, Mary, was a charming, white-haired Irish-American woman in her early sixties who had always been a homemaker. Her husband made a decent living as an accountant and had always been the breadwinner. Their kids were grown and gone. Mary's life was full of volunteer activities and grandchildren. After forty years of marriage, her husband had decided he wanted a divorce. Sad, but she had made peace with the idea, and at the settlement conference before the divorce master we were hoping to work out the last remaining points of contention. We agreed that Mary would keep the house, we agreed on how her husband's retirement account and pension were going to be divided, we agreed on the amount and duration of alimony, and we successfully negotiated some complicated health-insurance issues. We were done, as far as opposing counsel and I were concerned.

Enter the monkey wrench. There was one last detail. The parties had come up with a list of six paintings (which they acknowledged had no monetary value) currently hanging in their house, and they had decided that each of them would take three. They just needed to go down the list and pick. They easily agreed who was getting the first four, but when it came to the last two paintings, they both wanted the same one, which they referred to as "Fairy Tale." It was apparently a copy of a painting by some minor nineteenth-century artist. Mary told me that it was a picture of a little girl on a swing. Her husband had given it to her as a gift, and whenever she felt sad and in need of solace, she looked at it and it made her feel better. It was hers and she wanted it. Her husband said that "Fairy Tale" was given to him by a beloved aunt years before he and Mary were married, that he had never given it to Mary. He had simply hung it on the wall in their home. He wanted it.

Entire deal fell through. Despite the considerable pressure applied by their astonished and aggravated lawyers, neither spouse would back down on "Fairy Tale." In Mary's case, I think she felt that this was the last straw. She had no control over her husband's decision to divorce her, a decision she would not have made and one that was leaving her in a significantly worse financial position than she had expected to be in at this stage in her life. She had gone along with the program like the good Catholic girl she was raised to be, but this was where she was putting her foot down. He was taking away her future financial security and she was damned if he was also going to take away something that provided her with comfort during troubling times in her life, of which this divorce was probably at the top of the list.

Therefore, several months later, opposing counsel and I found ourselves at a conference in front of the judge who was subsequently assigned to preside over the trial of this matter. The judge asked us why we had been unable to settle the case. Given that this couple had no assets other than a house, a retirement account and a pension, it was an extremely reasonable inquiry before our clients embarked on a course of action that was going to involve the spending of a considerable amount of money, which they could ill afford, on legal fees. What she was really asking us was, "Are you crazy?" We explained "Fairy Tale" to her. Instead of exhibiting exasperated incredulity about what seemed to opposing counsel and me to be the absurdity of our clients' impasse, the judge nodded thoughtfully. Then she gave us a date to come back for another conference, this time with our clients. She wanted to speak to them before scheduling the trial.

The four of us came in on the appointed date. The judge took the bench. She told the court reporter that this was off the record; she just wanted to have a conversation. She asked everyone to sit down. Then she proceeded to tell our clients that she understood that a painting called "Fairy Tale" held so much meaning to both of them that it was the only thing preventing them from reaching a resolution of their divorce case. So, she said, she had decided to take a look at it for herself. The night before, she had gone to Barnes & Noble and found a book that featured works by the artist, including "Fairy Tale." She looked at the painting for a long time, thinking about why it might be so important to them. (At this point, opposing counsel and I were shifting uncomfortably in our seats and exchanging sidelong glances. This was not typical judge behavior and we had no idea what was coming next.) She agreed, she said, that it was a lovely painting and she could understand why they both would be sad to part with it. Then she asked each of them to tell her why they felt so strongly about keeping it. Mary, near tears, told the judge about looking at it when she was sad and how it helped her. Her husband told the judge that it had been given to him by his favorite aunt and it reminded him of her every time he passed by the painting. The judge listened carefully while they spoke. Then she told them that this was something they needed to try harder to decide for themselves. She pointed out that she was a stranger to them and would have no legal basis for deciding who kept "Fairy Tale." But she understood what an important decision this was, and she trusted them to figure it out. Then she scheduled us for a trial just in case and sent us away.

We never had to try the case. It settled. Mary got "Fairy Tale." Her husband got the other five paintings. There was nothing magical about this solution. Opposing counsel or I, or maybe both of us, had already suggested it, along with many other possible permutations, on the day the deal fell apart. The real reason we were able to settle was because the judge showed Mary and her husband such respect by acknowledging that this was a difficult decision for them. I think they felt heard. And that is so incredibly far from the typical family court experience. We were way more likely to have appeared before a judge who would have chastised them for wasting her time on trivial matters, one who would have given them a variation of my "I don't do furniture" speech, in an irritated, if not outright hostile, tone.

Mary was fortunate. I can only surmise that this judge must have something in her life that is the equivalent of my Christmas ornaments. She must have identified some important object in her own home that helped her empathize with Mary and her husband as they struggled to disentangle themselves from a lifetime of shared stuff, all embedded with memories and meaning known only to them.

Courtroom 7, 1:00 p.m.

Courtroom 7, sitting next to my client on a cold spring afternoon. Our support hearing was scheduled for 1 p.m., but the judge is handling bench warrants first, so we sit and watch. The room is bright and clean and new, up on the top floor of the suburban courthouse. Sun streams through the windows, illuminating the heads of three court personnel sitting in a row under the windows, doing nothing: one woman of about seventy-five, blond hair, Kelly green jacket; next to her, a slightly younger man with an enormous belly, wearing a court insignia on his lapel; and to their right, a sheriff, sweating in white shirtsleeves, belt heavy with holster, gun, and handcuffs, his hands encased in latex gloves. Sitting at counsel table on the side marked Plaintiff is the assistant district attorney; light brown hair, glasses, rumpled brown suit, early thirties, a tall stack of files rubber-banded together in front of him. He's fidgeting, shuffling papers, glancing around the courtroom, writing on his legal pad, breathing heavily. The judge's clerk sits at her desk, adjacent to the judge's bench, and reads a magazine. The court reporter is setting up her stenotype machine.

Everyone in the courtroom is waiting. Several are chewing gum. Everyone is white.

The door swings open and a second sheriff comes in, latex-covered hand on the elbow of the prisoner, whose own hands are cuffed behind his back. A stirring in the courtroom, the thin crackle of attention being paid. The prisoner is African American, maybe six-foot-two, late thirties, shaved head, chiseled features. He's wearing baggy sweatpants, sneakers, a pullover, and a miserable expression on his face. He's extremely handsome. A random thought flickers through my brain—this guy looks like a model. He could easily be in *GQ*, lounging in an Armani suit, instead of handcuffed in a courtroom. A white woman in pink scrubs and sneakers cries quietly in the back of the courtroom. The sheriff takes off the cuffs and pulls out a chair for the prisoner at the other counsel table in front of the Defendant sign. There are now two guys with guns and handcuffs on their belts standing behind the prisoner.

The ADA keeps his head down, riffling through files, making notes. The judge is nowhere to be seen. Without looking at the prisoner, the ADA starts talking. "Mr. Green," he says, "do you want the case continued to another date so you can have an attorney represent you or do you want to proceed without one?"

"If it's continued, do I go back to jail until the next hearing?" asks the prisoner.

The ADA doesn't answer. Everyone else in the room is quiet, the sheriffs, the court personnel who continue to do nothing, my client, me, the woman in scrubs. We are all listening. There's nothing else to do while we wait for the judge, and we all want to know the story.

"Have you spoken to the plaintiff?" the prisoner continues. "Did you call Julie?" The ADA says no, he has not spoken to Julie, but he knows that Mr. Green owes her over $5,000 in unpaid child support, that he is supposed to pay her $732 per month, that his last payment was made over three months ago and that was only for $300, that the total he's paid in the last year is only $1,200, and that the record shows a history of twenty missed court appearances.

"But we had an agreement, sir," says the prisoner. "I told her I can't pay $732 and she agreed that I could pay $300. She told me she would call here and take care of it so I wouldn't have to miss work."

No reaction from the ADA.

"Also, sir, I miss the court dates only because I can't take the time off from work. I always come in on my next day off and talk to the people. If you look in that file you'll see—I always come in. I just can't come when they're scheduled because if I don't show up at work I don't get paid or I could lose my job. That's why I came in today, because I couldn't come in last Thursday. I came in today to talk to the man and they arrested me."

The ADA, head still buried in the file, says that the child-support enforcement officer's recommendation is that Mr. Green pay $2,000 today, as a condition of being released. The prisoner rubs his eyes. "I don't have $2,000. I have $500 in my car which I'm supposed to give my landlord by 3:30 today or my family will be evicted. I have a wife and two kids and I'm the only one in the family working, sir." From behind me, I can hear the woman in scrubs start to cry again. "If I give you the $500 we'll be out on the street. If you put me in jail, I'll lose my job and I won't be able to pay any of my child support and my family will still be evicted. What am I supposed to do? Didn't Julie call you?"

"There's nothing in the record about the plaintiff contacting the court, Mr. Green. Do you want to proceed today without counsel or do you want a continuance?"

"Will I go back to prison if I ask for the continuance?"

A certain amount of sympathy is building in the courtroom. I can sense it. Perhaps it's the tiniest incline of heads toward the prisoner. Perhaps it's the complete silence that signals listening, the absence of any whispered conversation between the sheriffs, the lack of the familiar sound of the judge's clerk quietly turning the pages of her magazine.

In front of us, from behind the judge's bench, a door swings opens. The judge sweeps in, encased in floor-length black. She's in her early fifties, thin, with bangs and shoulder-length brown hair. All of us jump to our feet. The court officer with the enormous belly has miraculously sprung into action, calling court into session and introducing the judge. "Good afternoon," she says as she takes her seat on the bench, and we all respond, like characters in a well-rehearsed play, "Good afternoon, Your Honor." She tells us to be seated, we are, and she starts right in, energetic.

"Mr. Green, you can go forward with a hearing today without an attorney, or we can continue the matter to a later date so you'll have time to get counsel. Have you decided how you wish to proceed?"

I can hardly stand my mute observer role. I'm fighting an urge to jump over the barrier separating me from the counsel tables, run over to the prisoner and tell him what he should do. *Don't ask for the continuance! Go forward now! I know this judge, she's softhearted. You have a compelling story that you can tell as well as a lawyer would, and she can't incarcerate you for failure to pay child support unless you have the ability to pay the $2,000 right now. If she finds that you really don't have it, she can't put you in prison for not paying it. Nobody's explained that to you but that's the law. And even though no one's answered your question yet, your instinct about the continuance is totally correct. If the hearing is continued for you to be assigned counsel, you will be kept in custody until the next court date. And your family will be evicted and you will lose your job and there's just no advantage whatsoever to waiting. You are more than capable of telling your story to the judge. You're handsome and articulate, and your wife is here crying in the back of the courtroom.*

I hold my breath. The prisoner rubs his eyes and his temples. He shifts in his seat, then sits silently for several seconds. Slowly, he starts to talk, telling the judge that he figures he has nothing to lose by going forward with the hearing now because if the case is continued he'll sit in prison and lose his job, and his family will be evicted, so he'll take his chances. I exhale. "Very well," says the judge, and directs the sheriff to give Mr. Green a form to sign waiving his right to counsel at today's hearing. He signs and hands it back. The court officer puts a Bible in front of him and asks if he solemnly swears to tell the truth.

"I do," says the prisoner. The judge immediately turns to the ADA and asks him what he's asking for.

The ADA finally looks up. With a certain laid-back delivery which I take as a not-so-subtle signal to the judge that he is less than passionately committed to putting this guy away, he stands and recites the case history, including the pitiful track record of payments over the last twelve months, the many missed court appearances, and the enforcement officer's recommendation that the defendant be required to pay $2,000 as a condition of his release today. The judge turns to Mr. Green and launches into a rapid-fire series of questions.

"Who do you live with?"

"My wife and two children."

"Are you employed?"

"Yes."

"Where?"

"Harry's Café."

"What do you do?"

"Server."

"How much do you make ?"

"About $500 a week in tips."

"Do you get a paycheck, too?"

"Yes, but I get restaurant minimum wage and they take out taxes on my tips from that, so my check is usually, like, zero."

"Why haven't you paid your child support?

"Because I can't afford $732. I don't have it."

"How are your kids supposed to eat?"

No answer.

"You have four kids, two with plaintiff and two with your wife?"

"Yes, Ma'am."

"Whose responsibility do you think it is to support them?"

"I want to pay, your Honor, but I just can't afford $732 per month. And Julie knows I can't afford it. My oldest just turned eighteen and Julie agreed to reduce my support to $300 and she told me she would take care of the paperwork."

"Right now the order is $732 per month and the Assistant District Attorney tells me you've only paid $1,200 this entire year and you haven't made a payment for over three months. If I saw that you were trying to pay something every month I might feel differently about this, but you're not even trying."

"Ma'am, I want to pay, I just can't. I can't pay all my bills. We're being evicted because of rent we owe. I'm trying to get a second job but right now I only have the server job."

"Does your wife work?"

"She lost her job."

"How much is your rent?"

"Nine hundred thirty dollars."

"Do you have a cell phone?"

"Yes."

"Do you have any tattoos?"

"No."

"Do you smoke cigarettes?"

"No."

"Do you drink?"

"No, Ma'am, I'm a recovering alcoholic and I've been sober for five years."

"Do you have any savings?"

"No."

"How much money do you have?"

"I have $500 in my car that I'm supposed to pay my landlord today by three thirty. If he doesn't get it he's going to evict us. That's it. I don't have $2,000, Ma'am. If you order me to pay it I won't be able to and I'll go to jail and then I'll lose my job and my family will be evicted. I just don't have it."

I'm watching the judge. She's smiling at the prisoner. No way is she sending this guy to jail.

"Well, you seem like a nice guy."

No answer.

That's it. It's all over. She's going to let Mr. Green walk.

"If this order is too high for you to pay, you need to petition to modify it."

"I am going to, Your Honor."

"And if you reached an agreement with plaintiff for a lower monthly amount of support, you need to follow up and make sure that agreement gets entered into the system, okay?"

"Yes, Ma'am."

"So what I'm going to do is this. I want you to pay five hundred dollars today as a condition of your release from custody. Then you're going to have to pay a thousand dollars in two weeks, and I'm going to schedule a hearing two weeks from now."

"Your Honor, there's no way I can get the thousand dollars in two weeks. I'll be in the same place I am now and I'll end up in jail."

The same impulse I had earlier to jump the barrier recurs: *Be quiet! Don't argue with the judge. You just dodged a bullet. You're getting out of custody and anything could happen in two weeks. If Julie really did agree to reduce the order she can agree to accept less than the $1,000 in two weeks also. It's all up to her, really.*

"Well, that's my order. And if you can work something out with plaintiff in the meantime, fine, just make sure it gets filed with the court."

"Thank you, Ma'am."

One of the sheriffs motions for the prisoner to rise and put his hands behind his back. He does and they cuff him again. They're apparently going to keep him in captivity until he turns over the $500. His wife stands up, trying to approach him from the back of the courtroom, but the sheriffs awkwardly block her path. The prisoner twists his head back in her direction. "Call my mother," he says.

"Where's the car parked?" she asks. He tells her the cross street but she doesn't know where that is. He is trying to point with his head because he can't use his hands. She doesn't understand and she starts to sound panicky because he's being led out of the courtroom. At that, the sheriffs shed their impassive jailer expressions and become helpful guys from the neighborhood, giving the wife directions to the car.

"You can't miss it," the prisoner tells her. "It'll have a ticket on it." Funny, I think. Do other people? No one laughs. The wife follows along as her husband is led from the courtroom, latex-covered hand on his elbow.

"Where's the money?" she asks.

"In the glove compartment. Call my mother."

• • •

COMMOTION OVER, NO longer transfixed, I'm switching gears. Usually, I'm representing the Julies. Mr. Green talked a good game, but the facts were laid out by the ADA. He'd paid less than two months" worth of support over the course of a year. If Julie had really agreed to a lower amount of support, she would have told the court. If his wife had really lost her job, she would not have been wearing scrubs to court, she was clearly coming from work. And someone who wants to pay, but can't, pays a little bit every month.

But still. Even if he's not being honest about everything, this man's situation is horrendous. What's really awful is being poor. I try to imagine not being able to come up with $1,000 in two weeks' time. And even if it's not precisely true for Mr. Green, it's probably close. That means you have no one to call, no one in your inner circle has a savings account or a credit card. Not your brother, not your cousin, not your father-in-law, not your best friend. They're all living hand to mouth, like you.

And then there's the race thing. Regardless of whether his story has merit, there is something deeply disturbing about a room full of free white people centered around one black guy wearing, essentially, a leash and collar.

I look at my client, who seems unmoved. He was not, apparently, feeling sorry for Mr. Green or considering how handsome he was. And now he's nervous about the outcome of his own case. He's a salesman who earns about

$150,000 a year. His wife is a buyer at Nordstrom's and we're here to resolve a dispute over the amount of support he should pay for their three kids. Like me and my family, my client and his family inhabit such a different world from Mr. Green's. We own our houses. We renovate our kitchens, we landscape our yards, we take trips to Europe. Our kids will go to college. We will not be evicted. If my client needed to come up with $2,000, he could write a check. I'm quite sure he's never been in handcuffs.

The judge looks up and calls our case. We approach the bench and seat ourselves at counsel table, defendant side. The blond woman and the overweight man in shirtsleeves settle into their chairs. The court reporter replaces her paper, checks her phone. I'm done being an observer; now I'm in the play. I take the exhibits out of my file and organize them in front of me. I pour myself a cup of water from the pitcher on the table. "Call your first witness," says the judge.

AT DINNER THAT NIGHT, I tell my husband about Mr. Green. I tell him about the serving job and the eviction and the wife crying in the courtroom and the fact that the guy showed up voluntarily at the courthouse and got arrested. Not a flicker of sympathy. "Jesus," Alan says. "What was that guy thinking? Why'd he have all those kids? He should have kept his pants on."

On Being a Divorce Lawyer

My client is Daniel, father of the year to two adorable (he showed me pictures on his iPhone within five minutes of our first meeting) red-haired and freckled little boys, ages seven and eight. His wife recently moved to Toronto for a job that was too good to pass up. Their marriage had been shaky but this job was going to help. The biggest source of stress in their relationship, Daniel thought, was mounting debt, a house on the brink of foreclosure, and Alissa's unemployment. It was going to be temporary. Alissa was in Canada on a two-year contract, and then she would return.

The plan was to enroll the kids in school in Toronto but have them come back to Philly for their summer vacation, their winter and spring breaks, and a long weekend every month. Daniel wasn't happy about it, but it was only for two years, and he reluctantly decided it would be best for their family in the long run. The thought of not seeing his boys every day, of not reading them stories at bedtime or going to their soccer games or taking them on their Saturday morning just-us-guys trips to the barber shop was gut-wrenching. But he couldn't leave his job here; he had financial responsibilities to his family. So he decided to take one for the team.

Three weeks after Alissa moved to Canada, she filed for divorce and for custody of the boys. And now, several months later, she says she may not move back. Apparently there's a boyfriend in Toronto. And she's changed her mind about the summer; she told Daniel she thinks it would be better for the kids to come "visit" him (that term as applied to his boys makes him see red) for three weeks in July. She says they need the rest of the summer in Toronto to attend camp with their new friends. He is beside himself.

I show up in court stoked by the righteousness of my cause. We're here for the initial custody hearing. The summer is almost upon us and we have flatly refused to negotiate the "three weeks" position. I've handled lots of cases involving relocation and I am confident that the court, under these circumstances, will give Daniel custody for the vast majority of the kids' summer vacation. Not only because there doesn't appear to be one negative thing Alissa can say about his parenting, but also because he's such a sympathetic character in this unfortunate tale of marriage gone wrong. In telling the story, she looks bad and he looks good. Her lying (or, to be charitable, changing her mind immediately upon arrival in Toronto) may have nothing to do with what summer schedule is really in the best interest of the boys, but judges are human, and everyone's going to ache for Daniel. I certainly do and I suspect Alissa's attorney does, too. When I first spoke with him right after Daniel hired me to handle the custody hearing, he let out a sigh when I started talking. A sigh that meant, Oh man, this case. I could just feel it. He's a very good lawyer, I know him well, and he's not the type to say anything disloyal about his client. But he's a dad and a decent human being, and who wouldn't feel like Daniel's getting screwed here?

We have time before the hearing to negotiate. The four of us go into a small conference room adjacent to the court waiting area. It's a depressing place to hold such a serious conversation. The wood-grain contact paper covering the table is blistered and peeling, and one of the chairs is broken. Alissa starts talking, nervously picking at the curled edge of the contact paper. She raises questions about Daniel's work schedule during the summer, his ability to get the boys to camp and pick them up on time, the possibility that he may have to travel for business. We're prepared. I have Daniel lay out the whole summer plan, which includes soccer camp with the boys' friends from the neighborhood for two weeks, a week's vacation in Vermont, back to Philly for swim camp, etc. He does a great job. I'm polite and businesslike. At one point Alissa says she is just worried because the boys need to be at "home" during the summer. Daniel looks like he's going to jump out of his chair, so I say, a bit icily, "They have two homes now." She doesn't say anything. I tell her and her lawyer that we will agree to Alissa having the boys for a week after school ends and two weeks before it starts up in the fall, and that Daniel would be willing to have her come to visit with the boys for a weekend in the middle of the summer. She could even stay at the house, he says. But we will not agree to limit his time to three or four or even five weeks.

Daniel and I leave the conference room so that Alissa and her lawyer can confer. An hour later, they're still in there. I tell the court officer to take other cases ahead of ours because I'm hopeful we'll soon have a settlement. Alissa's lawyer comes out and motions me to meet him in the hallway. I know that he knows I'm going to win this one if we appear before the judge, and he's trying to convince his client of that. He also knows—because this is what he would do if he were representing Daniel—that once we go in that courtroom, I'm going to ask for the entire summer with no bookend weeks for Alissa and no visit in the middle. He can win those concessions for his client if we settle, but there is a substantial risk that he won't get either of them if we have the hearing. I tell him time is running out and we need to go into the courtroom. "I'm working on her," he says. "Give me ten more minutes." Twenty minutes go by. They emerge. "Okay" is all the lawyer says to me. Alissa looks tired and resigned. We tell the court officer we have an agreement, we go into the courtroom, and we put it on the record.

The following day pink tulips arrive at my office from Daniel. Two days later my husband tells me that a colleague of his, whose wife knows Alissa, heard through the grapevine that Alissa was upset about the outcome of her recent custody hearing, that her husband's lawyer was a real bitch, and that her lawyer wasn't very good. Apparently, the colleague's wife had asked the name of the bitch lawyer and found out it was me, so she told her husband, who told my husband.

So is that good? Is that bad? Who do you want your divorce lawyer to be? I'm not a bitch and Alissa's lawyer is highly skilled. But I know exactly why Alissa was dissatisfied with her lawyer, and I have been in his situation. I have had unhappy clients. I have been accused of "not playing hardball" and being a "Girl Scout," and I have been fired for being "too nice." Because Alissa's lawyer was pushing her to settle for what we were offering, she felt that he wasn't listening to what she wanted. She felt that he was not being a strong advocate for her, that he was weak, and that he let me dominate the outcome.

To the contrary. Alissa's lawyer was doing what good lawyers do. He knew the law and the judge we were about to appear in front of, he calculated the odds, and he concluded they were not good. By pushing her to take our offer, he was very effectively advocating for her interests. I can imagine just what went down during his lengthy discussion with Alissa in the conference room. He said, Let's take the compromise, the three weeks in Toronto and the mid-summer visit, and go home. Let's not risk losing more. And Alissa perceived that as caving in. She wanted him to say, Let's go get 'em. And some lawyers would have; some would not waste any time pushing the settlement, they would just shrug their shoulders and say, Okay, let's let the judge decide. And if it didn't go their way, which it probably wouldn't, Alissa would blame the judge, not the lawyer. It takes more sophistication as a lawyer, more investment in what is really in your client's interests, and more backbone, to push her hard to settle in a situation like this. In this instance, you're the one taking it for the team—you know your client will be unhappy, but you think she'd be unhappier if the case went to trial.

And Daniel? He thought I did a great job. He felt so validated when I reminded Alissa in our four-way negotiation that their sons had two homes. But really, that had nothing to do with the outcome. That was just theater. I had the winning case on the facts, and both lawyers knew it. Had we switched clients, the outcome would have been the same.

We divorce lawyers get a bad rap. Not only do many lawyers in other practice areas think what we do is messy and unpleasant, but lots of nonlawyers seem to view us as amoral home wreckers. A recent blog post I wrote regarding my sincere but ironic observation that most divorce lawyers I know personally place a high value on marriage drew more than a hundred comments, almost all of which were some variation of rant against us as opportunistic, unethical, and money grubbing. For example: *"Divorce lawyers see you as 'Billable Hours' and will do whatever is necessary to keep the gravy train rolling."* Ouch. This may be an accurate assessment of some of my colleagues, but it's more likely, I think, to be a projection of the unhappiness of divorce onto the lawyer; it's the Alissa scenario. After all, Alissa and Daniel both had to pay their lawyers a lot of money for that long and emotionally charged morning at the courthouse. She didn't get what she wanted, but her lawyer had to do just as much work as I did. So she has the double whammy of a big bill for something she is deeply unsatisfied with and didn't want to buy in the first place. I understand. I wouldn't want to pay my hourly rates either.

Consider the scene at my paralegal's wedding last year. Our whole office—lawyers and support staff—are invited. To a woman, we beam as she walks down the aisle; we collectively pull Kleenex from our purses as she ascends to the altar; we dance at the reception, a wild circle of us, frenzied with laughter, champagne, and excitement. Aren't we divorce lawyers? Aren't we supposed to be deeply cynical? Shouldn't we be so blinded by the dark side of marriage that we can no longer see beauty and hope in a wedding?

Emphatically, no. I am convinced that many of my fellow members of the family law bar place a high premium on marriage and family. We have an intimate knowledge of the importance of marriage in people's lives, because we have a unique window into the depth of the pain when it doesn't work out. We see up close how divorce makes people miserable, how it can play to the worst side of their nature, how it can make otherwise good people greedy or violent or destructive to themselves and their kids. And we also see the incredibly powerful draw of marriage. Despite the misery, so many of our clients navigate the choppy waters of divorce, land on the other shore, and then, often right away, they remarry. And look at the marriage equality movement. Our gay and lesbian clients and friends have been fighting for years for the right to join the ranks of the married.

There may also be an element of self-selection. Perhaps we find these issues so compelling precisely *because* we are so interested in all things marriage and family. Although some clients undoubtedly associate us with a low point in their lives and never want to see us again, many are really appreciative. The tulips from Daniel were great, and not all that unusual. At my firm, we receive lots of flowers. And candy. And thank-you notes. We are invited to weddings and baby showers; years after our representation ends, some clients continue to send us holiday cards and family photos. I love that. I want to know that my clients are enjoying their families, however those families have been reconfigured.

But it is understandable that we can become lightning

rods for anger and hurt more accurately directed at the opposing party. We become the bitch or the pit bull (which has
replaced "shark" as the lawyer/animal metaphor of choice).
This can be difficult. I hate running into my clients' exes
in the grocery store or on the train or, worse yet, at a dinner party. I duck my head. I'm glad my husband does the
grocery shopping because our local food co-op is chock full
of my clients' spouses, who would glare at me as I try to
grab the best asparagus and get out of there. (I might see
my own clients, too, who sometimes have the terrible idea
that I would like to update them on the latest developments
in their cases, despite my intense focus on the fingerling
potatoes.)

When my older daughter was in fifth grade, her base-
ball coach turned out to be the ex-husband of a woman I
was representing in what had become a very nasty custody
case. I imagined my daughter languishing in the outfield
and never getting up to bat. I dreaded the awkwardness
of interacting with the coach at practices. And I couldn't
say anything to my husband about it, because that would
have involved disclosing the identity of my client, which I'm
ethically prohibited from doing. Turns out, my fears were
unfounded, and I have to give the coach a lot of credit. Not
only did he refrain from sticking my daughter in the outfield
for the whole season (although that's probably where she
belonged, given her total lack of aptitude for the sport),
but he acted as if he didn't even know me. He completely

separated our roles as coach and parent from father and ex-wife's lawyer in custody battle. I have to say it made me see him in a different, and much rosier, light. More testimony to the fact that although people going through divorces or custody fights may behave horribly to one another, they can still be decent people in other aspects of their lives. In some cases, anyway.

I certainly didn't grow up dreaming of becoming a divorce lawyer, or any kind of lawyer at all. In fact, the only lawyer I was aware of as a kid was my father's college roommate (nicknamed Moon) who did my parents' taxes, which didn't strike me as interesting in the least. My parents were writers. All the adults I knew growing up were writers or worked in some aspect of the publishing industry. I decided at an early age to do something decidedly nonliterary: I was going to become a professional musician.

I had started playing the violin at age eight, and by high school was sure that it was my calling. I spent two disastrous years after high school in conservatory or, more accurately, in practice rooms at two different conservatories. I did not find learning to play an instrument really well to be a creative process. It's more like training for the Olympics. Most of it is rote drill. I didn't like it and it was almost immediately clear that I wasn't good enough at it—I was struggling to hold on to an orchestra seat in the back of the second-violin section. When I finally dropped out of music school, it was a humbling and emotionally brutal experience. I had picked a career, worked extremely hard at it, and failed. All by the age of twenty.

I found myself in law school several years later. It was mind-blowingly interesting to learn how the world worked: property and contracts and torts all seemed like secrets understood by powerful people who made things happen and I was now being given a membership in the club. In particular, I ate up Constitutional law. Reading Supreme Court opinions was and is one of the most intellectually engaging activities around; tax, corporations, secured transactions (just knowing what that meant was exciting to me, which is surely a sign of legal geekdom). I loved it all. When I heard classmates discussing how hard or competitive law school was, I told them they should try music school. Compared to my unhappy conservatory experience, law school was a cake walk.

I came to family law by way of feminism. Reproductive rights, employment discrimination, domestic violence— these issues called out to me, as they did to so many other young women who flooded law school classrooms in the late 1970s and early 1980s. I went to work at a firm that did employment discrimination and family law and quickly discovered that although I enjoyed the legal issues, I was not at all suited to the practice of the former: big, slow cases full of boxes upon boxes of documents; motions limping through federal courts at glacial speed. I preferred a different pace, and family law was a good fit: lots of cases, lots of different types of clients and lots of time spent with them, negotiations, trials (my performance skills served me well in this arena), writing, research. No two days were the same.

My partner, Joni Berner, and I met when I was working for a domestic violence organization, back when I represented Darlene in the ill-fated case where the judge gave custody of her baby to her boyfriend's parents. I recruited Joni to be on our legal advisory board. I remember going to her office, just Joni and a male secretary, which I thought was very cool, using Apple computers, which I thought was even cooler. She was just a few years older than I, and had worked for a large Philadelphia firm for six years doing plaintiff's-side asbestos litigation and family law. She had a baby, went back after her maternity leave, took a hard look at the old boy culture surrounding her, and said, I'm out of here. Taking twelve family law cases with her, she set up shop near her house in Center City. I also learned that she and I both had three-year-olds at home and were pregnant with our second children.

A year later, the funding for my position at the domestic violence organization was about to run out, and Joni, whose practice was taking off, offered me a job. I loved the idea of working with her but was unsure about going into private practice. I knew little about the economic aspects of divorce, having been focused solely on domestic violence and custody cases up to that point and having represented mostly people with no money. Would financial issues be interesting? Little did I know how much I would come to think so. And then there was the pesky question of men: Did I want to represent them? Not in domestic violence cases, I didn't. But what about as clients in divorce cases? I wasn't sure. (Although I overcame this hesitation almost immediately and have happily represented hundreds of men, my mother, until the day she died, always acted surprised when I used a masculine pronoun to refer to a client. "Honey, I didn't know you represented men," she would say, with a note of gentle reproach in her voice. Clearly, she had me pegged as a much more radical feminist than I turned out to be.)

I started working with Joni and her secretary, Tom, sharing an office at first, and then moving to a larger space, the first of three offices designed by my husband. Shortly after starting to work together, Joni and I became partners. We tried to build an office culture that fit us as mothers. We worked from home, at night, on weekends; we took time off during the day for school trips and volunteering in the classroom. We began to expand; we hired a paralegal, an associate, a law student. We moved into office number two; my birthday present that year from Joni was a big plush purple sofa for our massive new conference room. We had no dress code. We brought our children to work. Our employees brought their children to work. In the summer Tom wore shorts, which we were sure were really a bathing suit. Tom took his lunch hour from two to three p.m.

without fail (even in the middle of a deadline, much to our disapproval) so he could go to a local gay bar and watch *All My Children* with his buddies.

We knew what we wanted: to practice family law in a high-quality way, to represent a wide spectrum of clients, not just affluent ones, to have fun while still making a living. It was the making a living part that turned out to be so challenging. They don't teach you how to run a business in law school, that's for sure. Initially, we went into serious debt because we represented way too many people who either couldn't or wouldn't pay us. Eventually we toughened up, but there's still a thread of the tension between fun/good/interesting on the one hand, and rent/salaries/partner draws on the other hand, that runs through every decision we make.

Joni and I went through many difficult times, including witnessing the slow decline and ultimate death from AIDS of our beloved Tom, having our office manager of seven years walk off the job one day and refuse to ever see or speak to us again for no reason we could ever discern, and having a series of federal lawsuits filed against us by a crazy prisoner, the ex-boyfriend of one of our clients. We soldiered on, moved to a fourth and even bigger office, and added a third partner, the fabulous and indomitable Megan Watson, and several associates, all women, all practicing family law. As our children grew, we hired them. I can't think of a school-age child of mine, Joni's, or any other

lawyer's or staff person's who has not worked in our office.
A shredder is awesome entertainment for an eight-year-old,
and learning to answer a phone "Berner Klaw and Watson,
may I help you?" is a great job skill for a fifteen-year-old.
And anyway, it's cheaper than hiring a sitter.

WHEN YOU MAKE a living watching people who
were once in love be incredibly nasty to each other, it tends
to put any small problems and differences you have with
your family members into perspective. I am sure that dealing with the day-to-day strife in my clients' lives has made
me a better spouse. It also, I think, has made me a better law
partner. The similarities between the two relationships are
striking. I look at it this way: there's Alan, whom I met on
my first day of college and to whom I have been married for
thirty years. I spend evenings, weekends, and vacations with
him. We've raised two children together, with all the love
and commitment that entails. And there's Joni, with whom
I've been practicing law for twenty years. I spend my days
with her. Building a law firm also entails an awful lot of
love and commitment. Throughout the years we've added
many "children": associates, support staff, a new partner,
and scores of law students and baby lawyers whom we train
and mentor and generally fuss over and then proudly send
out into the world to fight the good fight.

The point is, the more emotional combat I see, the more
I mellow out with the people who matter most to me. The

more fighting I have to engage in on behalf of my clients, the less discord I want to take on at home or in the office. If I'm irritated because Alan can't find his wallet *again* or because Joni is late getting her bills out *again*, I just sigh and shrug. So what? I take the long view: This too shall pass. Which has translated into a combined total of fifty years of marriage. I'm thinking that maybe marital longevity is an occupational hazard of being a divorce lawyer.

Jimmy and Kaitlyn/ Interview in Chambers

The children are not my witnesses or Francis's witnesses. They're the court's witnesses. In Pennsylvania, it's up to the judge whether to interview children in a custody case, regardless of the parents' preference. And except in certain limited circumstances, usually involving much older kids, children don't take the witness stand and testify in front of their parents. Children are interviewed in the judge's chambers, with a court reporter and both attorneys present. Some judges ask counsel to waive their right to be there. Clearly, the fewer strangers in the room, the better the chances of the child's feeling comfortable. That's the obvious reason.

The less obvious reason is that if the lawyers are there we will inevitably go back into the courtroom and our clients will ask us what their kid said and we have to tell them—they're our clients. An experienced judge knows that in this scenario, the potential for parental shenanigans is huge. The parent who was not favored in the interview might retaliate against the child ("Fine, so if you want to live with Daddy you can just go there right now and you'll never be able to come to my house") or attempt to curry favor with the child ("When we come back to court, tell the judge you didn't mean it when you said you wanted to live with Mommy, because if you come live with me, we'll get a puppy"). No, I am absolutely not making this stuff up. Ask any divorce lawyer.

In our case, the judge will interview both kids, because at this point the determining issue in the case hinges on what Jimmy—and possibly Kaitlyn—says. There is nothing in the record linking Brian to the injury other than our having (hopefully) established that it occurred during Jimmy's overnight visit with Brian from Wednesday, February 22, to Thursday, February 23. We do have testimony from Brian that corroborates the spilled grape juice incident, which is helpful, but we have presented no evidence establishing that Jimmy sustained the bruise during that incident or that the bruise was caused by Brian's intentional act, rather than accidentally.

I am optimistic that we've laid the groundwork for Judge Diamond to have concerns about Brian's temper and parental judgment (my guess is that he believes the testimony about the force-feeding incident—he appeared to be paying very close attention to that topic during both Beth's direct examination and Brian's cross), which could result in him keeping primary physical custody with Beth. But Beth is hoping for more. She's hoping that Brian's custodial time will be sharply curtailed, or supervised, or suspended altogether for a period of time while he gets treatment. At this point in the trial, our only chance of obtaining such a drastic result is if Jimmy or Kaitlyn tells the judge that Brian intentionally hurt Jimmy. I know this, Francis knows this, and the judge knows it. I'm not sure if Beth understands it, but if she doesn't, that's just as well. I don't want her to feel that there is any more pressure on her kids. She is already agonizing about their having to talk to the judge in the first place.

Jimmy and Kaitlyn are out in the hallway with Beth's sister. The judge tells the court officer to go bring Jimmy around to his chambers through the hallway. I know he's doing this to avoid having Jimmy march through the courtroom in front of his parents, who are sitting at their respective tables, silent, waiting. He motions to counsel; Francis and I grab our legal pads and pens and follow him through the door behind the bar of the court, into his chambers.

Judge Diamond has some nice digs. His chambers are huge. In addition to the standard desk and chair, he has a conference table and chairs on one side of the room, and on the other a separate sitting area with a leather couch, a coffee table, and a couple of armchairs. He tells Francis and me to sit at the conference table, and he has the court reporter sit with her stenotype machine next to the couch. He's setting it up so that he'll be on the couch, Jimmy will sit across the coffee table from him in the armchair, and the court reporter will be close enough to hear Jimmy. Jimmy's back will be to me and Francis, so the conversation should feel, to him, like a one-on-one with the judge. The judge takes off his robe and hangs it on a hook on the back of the door, transforming himself into a civilian in shirt and tie, no jacket.

There is a knock, a "Come in" from the judge, and the door from the hallway swings open to reveal Jimmy. Beth dressed him well for the occasion, and in his clean khaki pants and button-down shirt he looks like a miniature version of his dad. He's adorable, and everyone in the room, even Francis, smiles when they see him. This always happens when a child is interviewed: The gravity of the courtroom, the weighty adultness of it all, disappears for a moment. The adults automatically shift gears. We become the dad at the family gathering, greeting his nephew's friend, or the mom at the school picnic, meeting her daughter's classmate. We soften. And I always wonder: Are we shedding our courtroom roles and becoming, for this brief interlude, who we really are? Or is the mom-at-school-picnic persona just a role, too, no different from the courtroom one?

"Hello," says the judge, "you must be Jimmy." Jimmy nods, but hangs back by the door. "Come on in." Head down, looking at his blue sneakers, Jimmy slowly advances. Judge Diamond stands up and holds out his hand. "I'm Judge Diamond. Nice to meet you, Jimmy." Jimmy tentatively shakes the judge's hand but doesn't say anything.

"And this," the judge says, motioning to the court reporter, "is Ms. Sokolov. She has this really neat machine where she writes down everything we say."

"Hi, Jimmy!" says the young and peppy Ms. Sokolov. Jimmy barely looks at her and does not seem at all interested in the "neat" stenotype machine. Many children are, in fact, very interested in it, and it's a common opening for an interview with a young kid. Judge Diamond does not introduce me or Francis. He sits down. "Have a seat, young man." Jimmy climbs into the chair across from the judge and pulls up his legs, curling himself into a ball. I glance over at Francis, who's doodling on his legal pad. I know what he's thinking, because I am, too: This child isn't going to talk.

"So, Jimmy, do you know why you're here?" asks the judge. No answer. "I'm a judge, and my job is to help your mom and dad make some decisions. They love you and your sister very much and they want to do what's best for you, but they need a little help. So I'm going to talk with you this afternoon so you and I can get to know each other a little and we can chat about some things. It won't take long. But first, I want to ask you something. Do you know the difference between the truth and a lie?" This is standard fare. To qualify a young child as a witness, to be able to admit his testimony into the record and rely on it, the judge has to establish that he knows what it means to tell the truth and that he agrees to do it. This is the child's version of the courtroom oath. Jimmy curls tighter into a ball and doesn't answer. Ms. Sokolov is poised, her fingers on the keys. Everyone waits. Silence.

Judge Diamond switches tacks. "Jimmy, would you like to come look out my window here? I want to show you something." I wonder what he could possibly be thinking. As far as I know, there's nothing out there but a run-of-the-mill suburban courtyard. It looks like I'm never going to find out, either, because Jimmy still doesn't answer and still doesn't move. I see a flicker of impatience on the judge's face. The clock is ticking. The dad-at-the-family-gathering persona is starting to morph back into the judicial one. He can't even find out if Jimmy is competent as a witness, much less talk to him about his bruise or anything else. He tries a new approach. "Jimmy, do you know I met your teacher, Ms. Peres, today? She's a very nice lady and she told me that you love your school. Is that true?" Silence. "What's your favorite thing to do at school?" More silence. The ball that is Jimmy's arms and legs shifts slightly, but doesn't speak.

The judge looks at the clock. It's now 4:20 and this interview hasn't even started. He waits another few seconds, and then he's done. He stands and walks to his desk, picks up his phone, dials his courtroom, and asks Mr. Doyle, the court officer, to come back to chambers. He turns back to Jimmy. "Jimmy, looks like we're not going to be able to talk today, so you can go back outside. It was very nice to meet you."

"Okay buddy," Mr. Doyle says to Jimmy when he comes to collect him. "Let's go." Jimmy obediently uncurls himself and hops down from the chair.

"Good-bye, Jimmy," says Judge Diamond. "Good-bye, Jimmy!" says the enthusiastic Ms. Sokolov. Neither Francis nor I say anything since we were never acknowledged in the first place; we're busy pretending we're not there.

"Bye," says Jimmy in a surprisingly cheerful voice and walks out the door. He spoke! Does this mean he's finally ready to talk? I've got an opening here; I need to try to exploit it.

"Your Honor," I say, standing up from my chair, "sounds like the child might be ready to talk. Could you call him back and try again?" He looks at me. Now his impatience is tangible, and he shuts me right down. "No, counsel. We're done here. I've spent enough time on this. I'm going to meet with the girl now."

I AM NOT anticipating Kaitlyn's having anything to say about the bruise. She told Beth she didn't know how Jimmy got it, and she must have said the same thing to Ms. Williams, given the unfounded report. The best I can hope for from her would be some disclosure that corroborates Brian's bad temper or his abuse of Beth or the force-feeding incident. Something that could tip the scales so that Judge Diamond finds that the kids are better off spending most of their time with their mom, that could ground a finding that Brian's custodial time should be limited. At this point, I've let go of the possibility of proving an actual incident of child abuse.

Another knock at the door, another "Come in" from the judge. Unlike Jimmy, who was clearly dressed by Beth, my experienced mother-of-girls eye knows immediately that Kaitlyn picked her own outfit for today's occasion. She's a symphony of pink and purple, with sparkly sneakers and her wavy light brown hair held back from her face by a pink-and-black leopard-print headband. "And you must be Kaitlyn," says Judge Diamond. "Very nice to meet you." He holds out his hand.

"Nice to meet you, too," says Kaitlyn, who strides right over to the judge and shakes his hand like a guest at a cocktail party. That gear-shifting thing is happening. Everyone in the room is now smiling fondly at this sweet little girl who has such poise. "Have a seat," says the judge, motioning to the chair recently vacated by Jimmy. Kaitlyn sits and fidgets with her headband. Ms. Sokolov is introduced and politely acknowledged. Francis and I are, again, ignored completely.

"So, Kaitlyn, do you know who I am?" asks the judge.

"A judge?"

"Correct. I'm Judge Diamond, and usually I wear that black robe over there, but when I'm in my chambers, my office, I take it off. But I'm still a judge. Do you know why you're here today?"

"Because Mommy and Daddy can't agree where I should live."

"And who told you that?"

"Mommy. She said they can't agree so you would decide."

"Did she tell you anything about what would happen here?"

Judge Diamond is fishing, trying to find out something every judge wants to know from every child in every custody case: Was she coached by either parent about what to tell the court?

"She said you would talk to me and I should answer your questions."

"That's exactly right. Did she tell you anything else?"

"She said to tell the truth."

"And that's right as well. Which is what I was just going to talk to you about, Kaitlyn. What does it mean to tell the truth?"

"That's when what you say is true. When you don't lie."

"If I said that my robe there was red, would that be the truth?"

"No."

"What would it be?"

"A lie."

"And is it okay to tell a lie?"

"No, it's bad. You can be punished."

"By who?"

"By God."

"And who told you that?"

"My dad. He said God knows when you're lying."

"Did you ever lie to your dad?"

"No, but one time he said I was lying."

"When was that?"

"One time when I heard Jimmy crying and telling Dad to stop it, and I asked Dad what he was doing and he said nothing, and I said he was hurting Jimmy and he said he wasn't. And he said if I told that to Mommy it would be a lie and God would punish me."

"Did you tell your mother?"

"No."

"When did this happen, Kaitlyn?"

"One time when we were at Dad's house."

"Did you see Jimmy crying?"

"Jimmy and Daddy were in the living room and I was in my room. But then I came into the living room because Jimmy was crying."

"And what did you see?"

"Dad was making Jimmy clean up the rug."

"Do you know why?"

"Because he spilled juice on it."

"Why did you think your dad was hurting Jimmy?"

"Because he was leaning over him and like shaking him or something and Jimmy was screaming."

I'm flabbergasted. Kaitlyn did not tell this story to her mother, whom she lives with, or to a social worker whose profession is interviewing children, and now she's sitting in a room full of strangers with a court reporter taking down her every word, talking to an old guy she's never met before and singing like a little canary. Did Beth prep her? Or could it be that when Beth and Ms. Williams questioned her they asked her specifically about Jimmy's bruise and she didn't connect that to this incident? Or maybe she talked to Jimmy about this last night? Or . . . I don't know. In any event, it's amazing. She's on a mission to tell this story—the judge hadn't even finished his colloquy about truth vs. lie before she started. Francis is looking sideways at me with suspicion.

"Did your dad say anything else?"

"You mean to Jimmy?"

"To Jimmy or to you. When you said he was hurting Jimmy."

"No, he just said he wasn't and Jimmy was just having a tantrum because Dad was making him clean up the juice."

"Did you see your dad do anything other than what you just told me about?"

"No."

"Did your dad tell you that you would be meeting with me?"

"No. I haven't been at my dad's for a while."

"Have you ever met Ms. Klaw?" The judge gestured in my direction and Kaitlyn turns around. She looks surprised;

Judge Diamond's set-up was obviously successful in making Francis and me invisible.

"No," Kaitlyn says to the judge. "Hi!" she says to me and Francis. We both smile awkwardly but remain silent, continuing the charade that we aren't really there.

More fishing. Judge Diamond wants to see if I met with Kaitlyn, to see if I prepped her for this interview. I would never do that. There's a big controversy among family lawyers about whether we should meet with kids in custody cases. They are, after all, witnesses, and we have a duty to zealously represent our clients. So we should, the argument goes, at least know what they're going to say to the court so we can prepare our case accordingly. That's one school of thought. I adamantly belong to the opposite school. I think the potential for tainting a child's testimony is way too great. And in exactly this type of situation, I want the court to know that the child has not spoken to me, has not been to my office, has not been brought into the litigation process by me. (I don't feel this way about cases involving teenagers, especially those in which the child's preference is the primary driver of the case. In those instances I think it's necessary to interview the child to make sure that the preference is clear and well-articulated before my client spends a lot of time and money pursuing whatever custody schedule the child says he or she wants. But a fifteen-year-old is very different from an eight-year-old.)

"Kaitlyn, are there any other times you were worried that your dad was hurting Jimmy?"

So great to be a judge. You can ask all the leading questions you want and nobody can object. If I asked a witness that question, Francis would be all over it, and the judge would absolutely sustain the objection.

"Umm . . . not really. But Jimmy cries a lot when we're at Daddy's."

"Do you know why he cries?"

"'Cause he's bad sometimes."

"What do you mean by bad?"

"Like he doesn't listen to Daddy."

"And what happens when he doesn't listen to Daddy?"

"Daddy gets mad."

"What does he do when he's mad?"

"Like yells at Jimmy and makes him sit in time-out."

"What else happens when you're at your dad's?"

"We watch movies and we go shopping. Daddy let me pick out the furniture for my room and I helped paint it, too. And sometimes we eat at McDonald's."

"Do you do homework at your dad's?"

"Yes. I have all As."

More involuntary smiles from the peanut gallery.

"I bet you do," says Judge Diamond. I can tell he's heard enough. He glances at the clock: 4:50. He looks back at Kaitlyn. "Anything else you want to tell me?"

"No, thank you."

Everyone smiles again.

"Well, Kaitlyn, it's been a pleasure meeting you. You're a very bright young lady. And you know both your parents love you very much, right?"

"Yes."

"And they just want what's best for you. So I appreciate your talking with me. And by the way, Kaitlyn, everything you told me this afternoon was the truth, right?"

Kaitlyn nods. "Speak so Ms. Sokolov can hear you," says the judge. Just as Kaitlyn is saying yes, the patient Mr. Doyle appears in the doorway. "Okay, then, Kaitlyn. Mr. Doyle will take you back outside."

"Bye," says Kaitlyn, and the door closes behind her.

Looking at me and Francis, Judge Diamond says, "Well, counsel, that was informative."

This is a declaratory statement, not an invitation for a friendly postmortem of the interview. We nod but say nothing.

"Quite a mature young lady," says the judge.

Again, he's not inviting comment.

"It's almost five. We need to go back on the record." And with that, Judge Diamond puts on his black robe, opens the door to his courtroom, and disappears.

Sperm Donor v. Father

WHEREAS, Ann and Paula are life partners who have been in a loving relationship for ten years and have formalized their commitment to one another by entering into a civil union on June 14, 2009;

WHEREAS, Ann and Paula intend to raise a family together;

WHEREAS, Michael is Ann's brother and has a close relationship with Paula;

WHEREAS, the parties intend for Paula to be inseminated with Michael's sperm in the hope that Paula will conceive and give birth to a child or children who will then be adopted by Ann;

WHEREAS, the purpose of this Agreement is to set forth the parties' understanding of their respective rights and obligations with regard to any such child or children born from the insemination so that no misunderstandings arise in the future;

NOW, THEREFORE, each of the parties agrees to be legally bound, as follows . . .

What's going on here?

From Ann and Paula's perspective:

They wanted to have a child together. They decided that Paula will carry the child; she would be the biological mother. They had two choices. One was to go to a sperm bank and shop for an anonymous donor based on the profiles maintained by the bank. They could select for height, weight, eye and hair color, ethnicity, religion, educational and family background, interests, and talents. They'd know a lot of facts about him, but they wouldn't actually *know* him. They wouldn't see, touch, or smell him, they wouldn't hear him laugh or sing, they wouldn't see him cry, they wouldn't know how he reacts in a crisis or how he experiences joy. They wouldn't know his name and they wouldn't know how to contact him. They'd refer to him as "our donor" or "No. 1225" or by some private nickname. Depending on the type of bank, they might choose a donor who is willing to be contacted when the child turns eighteen. Or they may have decided that carries too much potential for confusion and disruption and opt for a permanent lockdown on the donor's identity.

What are the benefits of this choice? Total control. They would be the only two parents their child knows. They would construct the narrative about the donor and they would decide how and when or whether to share it with their child. The donor would never show up on their doorstep. He would never sue them for custody. Their child would have a father only in the purely biological sense; the individual would be an abstraction. There would be no specific man attached to that term, at least until their child turned eighteen.

Ann and Paula rejected this option. They chose the other one, the messy, complicated option. They wanted to know their donor and to have their child know him, too. They wanted both of them to be biologically related to their child, so they asked Ann's brother to be the donor. They loved Michael. They knew him really well, and they would be happy to have their child be like him. They knew how kind Michael is, how much fun he is at a party, how talented he is at picking up foreign languages, how great a cook he is, and how devoted he is to his dogs. They also knew his weaknesses and they accepted them. They knew he could sometimes be grumpy, that he was a lousy driver, that his athletic abilities were minimal. And, although Michael would not be their child's legal parent—Ann would adopt the child, and the birth certificate would name Paula and Ann as the parents—they wanted their child to know who his biological father was, to know a real live man, not a concept. They wanted three adults, instead of two, to have an intimate connection to their child.

What were they giving up, besides control? Certainty. They had no idea whether the agreements they made before the child was born would be enforced by the courts in the future. The law was changing, struggling to incorporate new family configurations like this one. Who knew how Michael would feel about their (his?) child? Suppose Michael decided he didn't like the way Paula and Ann were raising the child and believed he could do a better job? He could petition for custody. Despite their agreement that he would have no parental rights, the law is far from clear as to his status. And suppose the child, as a defiant sixteen-year-old, decided he was sick of explaining to everyone that he has two moms and what he really wanted was to live with his sort-of father. What would they do then?

From Michael's perspective:
He was jumping off a cliff. He'd never had a child. Would he be able to have a relationship with a little boy who might look and act so much like him, whom he might find himself loving in ways yet unimagined, and still accept that the boy was not his child in the traditional sense of the word? Would it be okay to have no guaranteed input into decisions about where his daughter would grow up or what she would do, no right to spend time with her? And what if he had other children? How would he explain this child to them, and vice versa? Then there was the financial risk. Suppose Paula and Ann fell on hard economic times. Or

split up. What was to stop them, despite their promises at the outset of this venture, from looking to Michael to help support the child? It was no secret that he would be the child's biological father. He could end up on the hook for years of child support he never intended or agreed to pay.

And yet. He loved his sister and he adored Paula. He was so flattered that they asked him to be the father of their child. He was sure they'd be great parents. And he may never have any children—he was forty and not married. This might be his one shot to pass on his genes, to help create a life, to experience the joys of parenthood, even in this limited, backseat way. So he decided to take the risk. The potential payoff seemed so great.

Who are my clients?

Ann, Paula, and Michael had many discussions, over the course of several months, during wine-filled dinners, over morning coffees, on the phone, and through email. They came to consensus on a broad outline of their future, but some of the details were hazy. They decided to hire a lawyer to help them think through those details, one who could draft a contract that would set out in clear, specific terms what each expected of the others. They wanted to create a blueprint for how their nontraditional family would work, and they hoped that, if one of them didn't follow the blueprint, the contract would be enforceable by a court. They asked me to be that lawyer. But I couldn't represent all three of them.

Stripped to its core, the transaction involved one parent wanting to waive the right to receive child support in exchange for the other parent giving up custody rights. Someone's buying and someone's selling. The price of Michael's giving up custody was Paula's not receiving child support.

Everyone was on board with this at the time, before a child even existed, but suppose they changed their minds in the future? If Michael wanted custody? Or if Paula needed money? They'd be adversaries—potentially bitter adversaries—with diametrically opposing interests. So when they asked me to be their lawyer, I told them that I couldn't represent the three of them. I was fine with representing both Ann and Paula; going into this transaction, their interests were perfectly aligned. They both wanted to become parents of this child and they both wanted the same things from Michael: his sperm and his assurance that he wouldn't assert any rights to the child. (Their interests could become adverse in the future, if they broke up and had a dispute between *themselves* about custody or child support. In that case, it would be a conflict of interest for me to represent either of them; they'd both have to find new counsel.) I needed to think about the contract from their perspective, and I needed to structure it as tightly as possible to make sure they got what they wanted. While I understood that the child-support waiver, the "price," was critically important to Michael and I fully intended to build it into the contract, he needed an educated eye to review the contract solely from his perspective, to make sure it protected him to the fullest extent possible. Michael would have to hire his own lawyer.

Writing a contract requires starting at the beginning of the transaction and breaking it down into a series of discrete steps (Michael donates sperm, Paula is inseminated with sperm, Paula gets pregnant, Paula gives birth, child grows up . . .). For each of these steps, Paula and Ann told me what they wanted to happen, we thought together about how to make it work the way they envisioned, and then I did that thing that lawyers do, that essential reason people hire us: I thought about what could go wrong at each step, about where this delicate construct could veer off course, and suggested the best way I could think of to protect my clients if it did.

Some of the questions asked and answered in the contract:

What did Ann and Paula need from Michael before he donated sperm?

Michael's sperm was going to be deposited inside Paula's body. She and Ann wanted to make sure that the insemination would be safe for Paula, capable of fertilizing her eggs, and not likely to produce a child with birth defects.

Therefore, Michael agreed to undergo testing for sexually transmitted diseases, for genetic disorders, and for fertility.

What would happen to Michael's sperm after he gave it to Ann and Paula?

Michael would donate sperm to Ann and Paula solely for the purpose of inseminating Paula. Understandably, he wanted to make sure they didn't give it to anyone else. They agreed, so we specified that in the contract. Ann and Paula also agreed that semen not used in the initial insemination would be frozen and could be used by Paula, and only Paula, at a later date.

Suppose the insemination caused an injury?

Michael was well aware that there are no guarantees in conception, pregnancy, and birth. He did not want to be considered at fault if, despite cooperating with the testing they wanted, some harm came to Paula or the baby. Or even, somehow, to Ann. My clients understood, and I drafted this: *Ann and Paula hereby hold Michael harmless for any physical or psychological harm caused to Ann, Paula, or any fetus or child resulting from Paula's insemination with Michael's sperm.* Plain English: If there's a problem, Michael's not responsible.

Who would be the legal parents?

Ann and Paula, not Michael. Paula, by virtue of being the biological mother, and Ann, by virtue of a second-parent adoption, meaning that right after the baby was born, she and Paula would together petition the court to permit Ann to adopt Paula's baby. Michael agreed that he would not oppose that request or take any action to interfere with it. He also agreed that he would not be identified on the birth certificate. They made a secrecy pact, to be broken only by mutual agreement, that all three would recognize Ann and Paula as the child's only parents. To underscore these commitments, I added language to the contract stating that Michael specifically acknowledged his understanding that he would not have any of the legal rights he would otherwise have as the biological father of a child, and that he would not seek any type of guardianship, custody, or visitation rights.

Who would be responsible for the child?

This is the flip side of the deal. Ann and Paula would be assuming sole responsibility for the child's care and financial support. They realized the importance of protecting Michael against a future change of heart on this point. I wrote: *Ann and Paula agree to hold Michael harmless for any support for the child and to indemnify him against any support obligation which may in the future be imposed upon him, despite the existence of this Agreement.* Meaning that if either woman reneged on this commitment and did look to Michael for child support—and if a court were to make him pay it—they'd have to reimburse him, dollar for dollar. At least, that was my intent in drafting that sentence;

those were the strongest teeth I could put into the contract. My concern was that a court might not, actually, absolve Michael from the payment of child support despite the clear terms.

What will they tell the child about Michael?

My clients and Michael anticipated that there would come a time when they wanted to tell the child that Michael was the donor. They were adamant that the decision if, when, and how to have this conversation must be made by the three of them. This was a true act of trust in one another, because this particular point is way outside the realm of the law. I could and did write it into the contract, but if one of them breached that provision and disclosed Michael's identity to the child without clearing it with the others, what remedy could a court impose to compensate the other two adults? None. The child would already know, and the damage, if there were damage, would have been done.

What kind of relationship would Michael have with the child?

This decision had to belong to my clients; otherwise the whole purpose of the contract would be compromised. They would be the parents and they would decide how their child's relationship with Michael would be initiated and how it would develop. However, since all the adults here did expect that there would be some type of relationship, and because this aspect of the deal was so important to Michael, I included this sentence: *It is Ann and Paula's intent at this time to encourage contact and foster a relationship between Michael and the child.* Note: This merely affirmed their intent. At that time. It did not contain an absolute promise. They could decide, for any reason or for no reason, to prevent their child from having any contact with Michael. As I wrote this, I thought that if I were Michael's lawyer, I would push to tighten up this language, to make a future in which Michael would see his child as a given, rather than a possibility. But I was not his lawyer and I never heard from her on this clause, so the contract stayed this way, giving my clients wide berth to navigate an unknown future.

What if Ann and Paula split up? Or Michael got married? Or any of them had other children?
After much discussion, the answer to all these questions was the same: nothing. All decisions reflected in the contract were meant to be forever. They were not intended to be affected by future changes in the family configurations of the three adults. I will keep my fingers crossed that this resolve endures. I can see so many possible junctures where alliances could shift, where economic circumstances might change, where secrets could be revealed in a flash of anger or passion or alcohol-induced intimacy. But is that really different from any other, more conventionally structured family?

Would this contract hold up?

Maybe. And maybe not. Ann, Paula, and Michael had to treat this document as a statement of their mutual understanding. They had to trust one another enough to believe that each of them would feel morally bound to follow it, because neither I nor any other lawyer could promise them with certainty that a court would enforce these terms in the event of a future dispute.

THE TRUTH IS that it's not clear to what extent courts will allow adults to contract away rights that essentially belong to a child. Children are not property, and courts have an affirmative obligation to act in their best interest. So, for example, assume a future where Ann dies, Paula becomes disabled, and there's not enough money to put food on the table for the child. Isn't there a good argument that under these extreme circumstances the court should look to the biological father to kick in some funds? Doesn't the child need to eat? And shouldn't that need trump all three adults' agreement, entered into under completely different circumstances, that Ann and Paula would never seek child support from Michael? Or think about this: Suppose Michael and the child end up spending significant amounts of time together and develop a strong bond, and then Ann and Paula have a falling-out with Michael and they cut off all contact between him and the child. Couldn't a court find that it is in the child's best interest to continue to spend time with Michael? Since Michael is the biological father, why should the child's relationship with him be viewed as less worthy of protection than any other child's relationship with his father, no matter what a group of adults agreed to before the kid even existed?

Despite the thorny nature of these questions, the law around the country is moving toward enforcing contracts that define the rights and obligations of parenthood, often divvied up among several people. In Pennsylvania, in a case called *Ferguson v. McKiernan,* our Supreme Court was presented with these facts: Mr. McKiernan was Ms. Ferguson's ex-boyfriend. After they broke up (and, interestingly, while she was married to someone else), she asked him to donate sperm for her to use for in vitro fertilization, as her tubes were tied and she wanted to have a child. She promised that she would keep it a secret and that he would have no financial or other responsibility for the child. He agreed, and twin boys were ultimately born. McKiernan was present at the twins' birth, but Ferguson put her husband's name on the birth certificate. Thereafter, the parties moved on with their lives. Ferguson eventually divorced her husband; McKiernan married, moved away, and had a child with his wife.

Out of the blue, when the twins were five years old, Ferguson called McKiernan and asked for financial help. He refused, and she petitioned the court to make him pay child support.

McKiernan challenged the petition on the basis that they had made an oral contract and she had waived her right to child support from him. He took this challenge all the way up to the state Supreme Court, because he lost the argument in the trial court and again at the first appellate level. Although the lower courts did agree that the parties had formed a binding oral contract that McKiernan give sperm in exchange for Ferguson's agreement to forgo child support, they declined to enforce it, asserting that Ferguson and McKiernan were attempting to bargain away a legal right that didn't belong to either of them. The right to receive child support belongs to the child, the lower courts said, and courts can't "ignore and callously disregard the interests of the unheard-from third party" (in this case, the twins).

McKiernan received a more sympathetic reception from the state Supreme Court. While giving a nod to the compelling you-can't-bargain-away-a-child's-rights argument, the court ultimately rejected it, preferring to recognize the reality of the lives of all the Anns and Paulas out there. They found that as more and more children are conceived through donor insemination, there are strong public-policy considerations favoring the use of known, rather than anonymous, donors. They listed, in fact, all the reasons Ann and Paula wanted Michael as their donor. A woman, the court said, "who cannot conceive through intercourse" (not quite the Ann and Paula situation, but close) should be able "to seek sperm from a man she knows and admires." In order for those men whom women "know and admire" to be willing to donate sperm without the protective cloak of anonymity afforded by a sperm bank, the court acknowledged that a valid, enforceable child support waiver is a necessary part of the deal. They reversed the lower courts and ruled that the contract was enforceable. McKiernan was off the hook for child support.

This was not a unanimous decision. The theme of the dissenting opinion was that calling McKiernan "Sperm Donor," which was how he was referred to in the majority opinion, does not change his status. He is, simply, the twins' father. The dissenting justice painted an improbable but disturbing picture. "The children point and say, 'That is our father. He should support us.' What are we to reply? 'No! He made a contract to conceive you through a clinic, so your father need not support you.' I find this unreasonable at best." But despite this protest, the decision to uphold the contract stands, and is, at the time I write this, the last word on the subject in Pennsylvania.

The outcome of *Ferguson v. McKiernan* would seem to insulate Michael. But suppose the next case to move up the appellate ladder after Ann and Paula's child is born involves a different set of facts? In another recent Pennsylvania case involving a separated lesbian couple, their donor, a good friend who had been an active participant in their children's lives, was awarded partial custody and made to pay child support. The court there clearly felt that those particular children had three parents, and they divided both the rights (custody) and the obligations (support) three ways. There will undoubtedly be more decisions on this issue, and a new law may be passed. So the ground continues to shift.

The Ann-Paula-Michael trio is only one alternative-family configuration. It can be more complicated. Consider this: Triplets were conceived via in vitro fertilization of a donor woman's eggs with the intended father's sperm, and the resulting embryos were implanted in a different woman, a gestational carrier, who carried them to term. There was no intended mother for these children; the contract between the father, the egg donor, and the gestational carrier provided that the father would be the only parent. However, after giving birth to the triplets, the gestational carrier, despite the contract she signed with the father, sought custody of them. Although she initially won, on appeal a Pennsylvania court overturned that custody award, finding that she had no legal standing—that is, no right—to seek custody, and the triplets ended up in the sole custody of their father. The father, in a really stunning display of let-me-rub-salt-in-your-wounds aggression, then petitioned the court to make the gestational carrier reimburse him for all the child support he had paid while the case was working its way through the courts. His argument was that since the court found that she didn't have standing to seek custody, she likewise had no standing to seek child support. The court, not surprisingly, did not agree. They found that because the gestational carrier was caring for the triplets, even if it was ultimately determined that she had no right to do so, the support benefited them during that time, so Dad was not entitled to a refund.

You can see from these cases what's happening. Courts are starting to sanction the idea that you can choose one aspect of parenthood but forgo others, and those choices will be legally binding. You can contribute DNA but accept no responsibility for raising a child, emotionally or financially. You can rent out a nurturing womb and agree that your connection to the resulting baby will be severed at the moment of birth. The tricky part for courts and legislatures is to find a reasonable balance between the right of competent adults to contract with one another as they please and our collective responsibility to protect the interests of children not born at the time those contracts are made, children whose need for care and support, once they are alive, is no different from that of any other children.

As for Ann and Paula, all I know is that healthy twins were born. Since I received the birth announcement, I haven't heard from them, which, in my business, is just about always good news.

Good Parent, Bad Parent

I was preparing for trial in a case in which my client was seeking primary custody of his eight-year-old son. Vladimir came to my office carrying a plastic bag filled with the clothes Nikolay had been wearing when he picked him up from school. Vlad was convinced that the contents of this bag would constitute airtight proof that his ex-wife, whom he hated with a Russian passion that appeared to know no limits, was a totally unfit mother. The bag included a pair of mismatched red socks with holes in the toes, a navy blue sweatshirt with frayed cuffs, dirty gray sweatpants, which he said were too short for the kid, and what Vlad considered the pièce de résistance: a pair of worn-down slip-on sneakers. "Look!" he said. "Not real shoes! She make child wear slippers to school!"

All I could think of, combing through the sad, wrinkled bag of little-boy clothes, was the long list of inappropriate outfits my children had worn to school over the years. To this day, my adult daughters wear mismatched socks, generally with holes in them; in elementary school they frequently went to class in ripped clothing because they were attached to it, and their father and I didn't care. Wear two dresses at once? Sure. Flip-flops in March? Probably would've gotten by us, as well.

So whose filter is the better one here? Should I introduce this evidence (have the slip-on sneakers marked Exhibit A for identification, hand them to the court officer to take up to the bench for inspection by Her Honor, and move for their admission into evidence) because my client thinks it's important? Even if the judge, a woman with a young son of her own, would be, in my opinion, unlikely to think it is? Will it actually make him look petty and thus undermine the importance of the real issues he has about his child not succeeding in school due to a way too casual attitude on the mother's part about regular attendance and homework? This can be a difficult discussion. There's certainly no one answer. I have to check my own parenting views at the door while I try to figure out the mainstream consensus, at least enough to advise my client what the judge may think is important.

Here are some examples of evidence that I talked clients out of introducing in custody cases: Mom buys the kid's clothes at the thrift store (so what, and complaining about it makes Dad look like both a snob and a cheapskate); Dad is an atheist (I refuse, on principle, to argue that a child is better off in a religious household than a nonreligious one, and then there's that pesky First Amendment issue); Mom is a lesbian (absolutely will not go there); Dad's new girlfriend paints the four-year-old daughter's fingernails (what little girl doesn't want that done? And nail polish remover is cheap); Mom feeds the kids pizza three nights a week (she's a working single mother — of course she does, and any female judge with kids is likely to be sympathetic).

I nixed the slip-on shoes. I did, however, despite a certain amount of distaste at doing so, introduce into evidence the ripped-up sweatshirt, too short and dirty sweatpants, and mismatched socks with holes in the toes. I have no idea if they made an impression on the judge, but she switched primary custody to my client at the conclusion of the trial. I hope it was due to the strong case we presented concerning the great relationship Vladimir had with Niko, the attention Vlad paid to school attendance and homework, and the activities they enjoyed together, rather than the mother's propensity, much like my own, to let the child wear old or torn-up clothing. My client was sure that it was the introduction of the clothing as plaintiff's exhibit 3 — after the school attendance records, no. 1, and the reports cards, no. 2 — that cinched the deal. The judge didn't write an opinion, though, so we'll never know.

THE BASIC LEGAL standard applied to child custody cases in every jurisdiction in the United States is "best interest of the child." That is what the court is charged with determining when parents can't agree on where their children should live. Some states have laws that spell out, in elaborate detail, individual factors that judges need to consider in order to make that determination, such as evidence about domestic violence, other adults in the household, where siblings live, et cetera; other states leave it wide open so that the judge can arrive at her conclusion any way she chooses. No matter what kind of statute you're operating under, in the final analysis it comes down to a subjective decision by a judge (child custody cases are almost never heard by juries) about parenting. It comes down to the person in the black robe, who, given the age of most lawyers when they become judges, is most likely to be from a different generation than the parents in his courtroom, and may be from a different race, ethnicity, socioeconomic background, religion, and neighborhood, trying to decide what's best for a child he doesn't even know. And so much of it is informed by the judge's specific experiences: Did she share a bedroom with siblings? Did his wife work when their kids were small? Did her father use corporal punishment? Did he have to work in the family business on weekends?

I'd much rather be the advocate, not the decider. In ascertaining what's in a child's "best interest," how do you eliminate biases you harbor based on your own particular experiences, that it would be unfair to universalize, while drawing on the body of knowledge and common sense acquired during a lifetime of parenting, grandparenting, or even having been a child yourself? Some judges, unfortunately, seem blissfully ignorant of the complexity of this task, and don't appear to even try. Instead, they rely on this faulty syllogism: I was raised this or that way, I turned out great (I'm a judge!), therefore all children raised this or that way will do fine. Others try hard to be sensitive.

BREASTFEEDING IS A great example. It's pretty well accepted by the courts as a medical truth that breastfeeding has major health benefits for children. It is also the stated policy of the Commonwealth of Pennsylvania that children, including infants, benefit from spending time with both parents. Breastfeeding frequently and spending long periods of time with Dad are mutually exclusive. So how does a judge figure it out? Despite the availability of expert testimony on both the health benefits of breastfeeding on one hand, and on the psychological benefits of paternal bonding on the other hand, the judge is very likely to pull from his own knowledge about breastfeeding, which may be little to none, and his awareness of cultural norms. Of course, that's a changing landscape. But at this point on the cultural continuum, the mother who says her four-month old cannot be away from her for more than two hours at a time because that's how often he nurses and he won't take a bottle will be pretty convincing, and that will likely drive the custody schedule, meaning that Dad may get only two-hour visits for a while.

What about when the kid is eighteen months old and still nursing? By now, he's obviously eating solid food as well, but suppose Mom says he can't stay overnight with Dad because he needs to nurse in the middle of the night and she has difficulty pumping, and her milk supply will suffer. What's best for the kid, more breast milk or more time with his father? And when he's three? Is Mom weird because she's still breastfeeding a three-year-old or just making a legitimate parenting choice that, although uncommon in contemporary North American culture, should be protected by the court? And what if protecting it by the court means that Dad isn't able to take the three-year-old to visit his family in California for a week because that would have the effect of forcibly weaning the child?

Co-sleeping is another one of these issues. We all know that parents' sharing a bed with their children is the norm in much of the world, but it is not, apparently, in the small segment from which most contemporary American judges hail. I have had a number of cases in which clients wanted me to introduce evidence of the other parent sleeping with a child to show bad parenting. If it's a one-year-old, nobody thinks it's inappropriate, and if it's a thirteen-year-old sleeping with the opposite-sex parent, pretty much everybody does. So where do we draw the line?

What about a three-year-old? Specifically, what about a three-year-old girl sleeping in bed with her father during his custodial weekends? Seems logical to me that a child who hasn't seen her father for maybe ten days, and is not sleeping in her normal bed, would want to sleep with him for comfort and connection, and he may very much want that physical closeness as well, to make up for the inevitable loss of intimacy that comes from their living apart. And it's not just logic; I'm looking through my own lens. Alan and I thought nothing of letting our girls sleep with him during trips or camping, or just because one of them wanted to snuggle when she was sick or lonely or scared. I loved sleeping with my children and I loved that he was able to have the same delicious, animal experience.

But I have learned, because this particular issue comes up with great frequency, that my view of co-sleeping with young kids as positive or, at worst, benign, is definitely not shared by most of the judiciary before whom I appear. I can remember tender scenes of my sweet daughters snuggled up between me and their father in the dim groggy morning light as much as I want, but I have seen judges raise both their eyebrows and their voices when hearing of such behavior and specifically admonishing parents not to do it.

Same goes for parental nudity. Some parents flip out about the other parent showering with a child of the opposite sex (some, even a child of the same sex). Is this evidence I want to present to the judge to make him think Dad is, if not actually sexually abusive, creepy? It's hard for me to do it, since I don't think there's anything wrong with parents undressing in front of their children. I actually think it's a good thing to raise kids who are comfortable with nudity. But this, too, seems to be a distinctly minority view in contemporary American culture. Most parents I have represented think it's bad if the opposite-sex parent does it and most judges absolutely agree. This is really about trends, not law. Which parenting practices are in vogue and which have been discarded?

Take tattoos. In the early 1990s I represented a woman whose boyfriend, the father of their son, was a member of the Warlocks motorcycle gang. Part of the gang culture required getting tattooed with the Warlock colors, and this applied to women as well, although they could not actually be gang members (they were called "properties," no kidding). Before their relationship ended, Stacey had been a "property" of the Warlocks and she had numerous tattoos on her arms. I insisted she wear a turtleneck to court so that no tattoo would show, because I was very concerned that the seventy-something judge would feel that a woman tatted to the hilt could not possibly be a good mother. (This turned out to be a bit of an ordeal, as a turtleneck did not live in Stacey's clothing repertoire. It required a shopping trip to a department store I'm sure she hadn't seen before or visited since.)

I know I made the right call in that case. But how times have changed! Just think of all the elegant tatted mommies gliding down the streets of Park Slope or West Hollywood pushing their $1,000 strollers. No judge now would think a woman with a rose on her ankle or a snake on her wrist was unfit for the preschool carpool. And why is that? Because his daughter's covered with them! Maybe his wife even got one for her fiftieth birthday.

When Justice Sonia Sotomayor was seeking confirmation from the United States Senate to become a Supreme Court Justice, she was dogged by a comment she made years earlier at a law school conference about the value of having a "wise Latina woman" on the bench. Several Republican members of the Senate Judiciary Committee professed outrage about the notion that one's personal experience should have any bearing on one's actions as a judge. To which any lawyer (with the apparent exception of those members of the Judiciary Committee), any judge, anyone who's ever been in a courtroom, and anyone who's ever even watched Judge Judy would say "Who are you kidding?" And isn't it obvious that we benefit from the subtlety, nuance, and judgment that come from spending the better part of a lifetime on earth? Otherwise, we could insert a set of facts and a legal principle into a computer and get a result.

In the speech, Justice Sotomayor described the interplay this way: " . . . in any group of human beings there is a diversity of opinion because there is both a diversity of experiences and of thought . . . [t]he aspiration to impartiality is just that—it's an aspiration because it denies the fact that we are by our experiences making different choices than others. My hope is that I will take the good from my experiences and extrapolate them further into areas with which I am unfamiliar. I simply do not know exactly what that difference will be in my judging. But I accept [that] there will be some based on my gender and my Latina heritage."

And that's the tension. If I hold up a pair of too-small slip-on sneakers and ask that the court consider them evidence of a mother's not acting in the best interest of her child, I expect the judge to call on her reservoir of knowledge and common sense, and that reservoir will almost surely be different for a single working mother judge than for a male judge whose wife stays at home and who neither shoe shops nor dresses the kids for school. That male judge has to be willing to be educated about something of which he lacks firsthand knowledge, and that female judge has to be willing to put aside feelings about little boys and their sneakers that might be particular to her own experience. In addition, both of them need to be able to discern the difference between mere fashions—are you really a better parent because you have no tattoos?—and substantive differences, like whether sleeping with your three-year-old is actually harmful or just uncommon. It's a delicate balance, for sure.

ANATOMY OF A TRIAL, PART VII:
The Ruling

After Judge Diamond finished his interviews with Jimmy and Kaitlyn, he took us back into the courtroom, where Brian and Beth were waiting, and told us that he would be adjourning at 5:00 p.m., which was then about two minutes away; closing arguments would not be necessary, as he had all the information he needed and he did not require anything further from counsel; he would not rule from the bench, because he wanted time to review his notes; the temporary order would remain in effect until he issued his final order, and he expected that order to be fully complied with (he looked sternly at Beth); and he was scheduling us to come back the following Wednesday at 9:00 a.m., when he had an opening on his list, at which time he would give us his ruling.

I was sorry not to give a closing. A closing argument is a lawyer's opportunity to be passionate and articulate, to find a theme and weave the evidence into it, to paint a complete picture. And it's a chance for the client to hear her case pled directly to the court. The lawyer is, finally, her voice, telling her complete story. If done well, it's satisfying to the client and, the lawyer hopes, persuasive to the court. If you're in front of a jury, it's an essential part of the trial. With non-jury cases, as in family court, it's expendable. Many judges I practice before think that closing arguments are superfluous; they've heard the facts, they don't need lawyers to spin them into a consistent narrative, and they don't have the extra half hour, anyway.

I was also sorry that Judge Diamond took the case under advisement for a week. It was the worst of both worlds. If a judge asked me (which he wouldn't), I'd happily trade off the opportunity to do a closing argument cobbled together on the spot for an immediate resolution of the case. But given that we had to come back in a week, I could have prepared a bang-up closing. Plus, I was sure to have a week of phone calls from Beth wanting to speculate about how the judge would rule and what we could have done better in the trial, neither of which topics I was looking forward to discussing.

THE FOLLOWING WEDNESDAY at 9:15, Francis, Brian, Beth, and I are all sitting at counsel table when Judge Diamond comes through his chambers door and takes the bench. He starts right in. "We're back on the record in the matter of *Foster v. Foster,* Mother's Petition for Custody. At the outset of this litigation, Mother sought primary physical custody of the children, with Father having partial physical custody on alternate weekends. Father has consistently sought an equally shared physical custody schedule such that the children are in his custody on alternating weeks. The court notes that prior to trial, the parties were operating under an agreed temporary order, worked out between counsel, which gave Mother primary physical custody and Father partial physical custody on alternate weekends and Wednesday overnights. However, at the outset of the trial, Mother amended her request for relief to ask that this court refrain from awarding Father any physical custody at all at this time—or, alternatively, permitting Father only supervised visitation—until Father has completed anger management treatment and parenting classes. The reason for this request is an allegation of child abuse made by Mother. I will address this abuse allegation first."

I can hear Beth inhale sharply. I put my arm around the back of her chair.

"In regard to the alleged abuse of Jimmy, this court heard testimony from Mother and from the child's preschool teacher, Ms. Peres, both of whom testified to seeing a large bruise on Jimmy's right arm after Jimmy spent the night at Father's. The court has also reviewed and admitted photographs of the child's arm, which were offered into evidence by Mother. It is undisputed between the parties that this matter was investigated by Child Protective Services, and in lieu of testimony from the CPS caseworker, the parties stipulated through counsel that the result of the CPS investigation was an unfounded finding, and the letter so stating was admitted into evidence. Additionally, Mother submitted the child to a forensic pediatric examination at Children's Hospital of Philadelphia, the result of which was not conclusive regarding the cause of the bruise. Father testified that he did not know how Jimmy obtained the bruise, and speculated that it could have occurred during the child's gymnastics class. He also testified that he did not use corporal methods of discipline with his children. Father's sister, Jessica Foster, who spends considerable time with Father and the children, corroborated that Father does not use corporal punishment.

"Finally, this court met with both children separately in chambers. Present during those interviews were my court reporter, Ms. Sokolov, and counsel for the parties, Ms. Klaw and Mr. DiLorenzo. As to Jimmy, who is five years old, despite considerable effort on the part of this court, no interview actually took place, as Jimmy was unwilling to speak at all and therefore the court was not able to ascertain whether he possesses the requisite understanding as to what it means to tell the truth. Because the court was unable to perform this necessary colloquy, the court did not question Jimmy regarding the abuse allegation or anything else, for that matter.

"Kaitlyn, who is eight years of age, and whom this court found to be a very articulate young lady, did satisfy the court that she understood what it means to tell the truth and confirmed that the statements she made in chambers were true. Unlike her brother, Kaitlyn volunteered a considerable amount of information concerning a recent incident in which Father required Jimmy to clean up juice he spilled on a rug in Father's home which, this court notes, is not inconsistent with Father's testimony that he corrects his children rather than physically disciplining them. In summary, while I find that Jimmy had a bruise on his arm and it is not disputed by Father that there was an incident involving Jimmy cleaning up spilled juice on a rug, I cannot find by a preponderance of the evidence either that Father caused Jimmy's bruise or, if he did cause it, that the cause was intentional rather than accidental."

That's it? No mention of Kaitlyn saying—I wrote it down in chambers—that she saw her dad leaning over Jimmy and shaking him "or something" and Jimmy was screaming? No tie-in to the force-feeding incident or the angry drop-off at preschool?

"I also heard extensive testimony from both parents and, as previously mentioned, from Father's sister. The court notes that the parties appear to have different parenting styles"—tears are starting to roll down Beth's face—"with Father being less concerned with consistency in routines such as bedtimes but more of a disciplinarian when it comes to 'house rules.' I also note that both parties described Jimmy as a very active little boy. Additionally, as with many divorcing parents, there were a number of negative allegations made by each party against the other, with Mother accusing Father of abusive behavior towards her and Father accusing Mother of being angry at him for an extramarital relationship, and so on. Suffice it to say, these parties are separated and in the midst of a divorce, and these accusations, whether true or not, are water under the bridge. This court is not persuaded that any of this testimony is relevant to the determination of what custody arrangement is in the best interests of these children, which has to be my sole focus.

"Therefore, I am going to deny Mother's request for an order suspending Father's partial custody and directing him to have any particular type of counseling. I find that both the children's aunt and Kaitlyn herself described a good relationship with Father and I see no reason to curtail Father's time with the children. On the other hand, the court acknowledges that Mother has historically been the children's primary caretaker and Father has admitted he is new to the role of taking care of the children on his own, and the children are still very young. Therefore, I am not going to order an equally shared custody arrangement at this time.

"I am going to award shared legal custody of the children, which was not in dispute, primary physical custody to Mother, and partial physical custody to Father on alternate weeks from Thursday after school to Monday morning, drop off at school, and on the off weeks, Thursday after school to Friday morning, drop off at school. This arrangement gives the children the benefit of a significant, uninterrupted block of time with Father every other week, while preserving a primary home with Mother, which I find to be in the best interests of these children at this time. Each party will have two weeks of vacation, upon thirty days' notice to the other parent. Regarding holidays, I urge counsel to try to work out a holiday schedule and submit it to the court for approval. In the event you cannot, each counsel should submit a proposed holiday schedule and I will enter an order based on the two proposals. Please have either the agreed-upon schedule or your individual proposals to me within fourteen days. I want to thank counsel for a well-presented case. Mr. and Mrs. Foster, you have two wonderful children and I urge you to try harder to get along, for their sake. I wish you luck. Please wait for a copy of the order."

IT'S OVER. DURING the past week, while we were waiting for the ruling, I tried to prepare Beth for the possibility of this result. I did relay what Kaitlyn told the judge in chambers, and I asked her outright if she had any conversations with Kaitlyn that might have prompted her to "remember" the grape juice incident. She said she didn't. I also told her that Kaitlyn said she did not see Brian squeezing Jimmy's arm, so there was still no direct evidence that Brian intended to injure Jimmy. So I don't think she's surprised at this outcome.

But she's angry. Beth feels so frustrated that no one—not Child Protective Services, not the pediatrician at the ER, not me, not the court—will protect her children from an abusive father. Jimmy said his father did it. And that he told him not to tell anyone. The fact that she wasn't allowed to testify to this still seems ludicrous to her. Her son confided in her, and she believes him. But the court doesn't, so he has to keep going to his father's house for visits, and now it's more dangerous than before because his father knows Jimmy told his mom and will find some way to retaliate against him. And probably against Kaitlyn, too. The laws are so unfair, designed to protect abusers. The more they threaten children not to speak, the greater the likelihood that they will get away with it. And, aside from the bruise on Jimmy's arm, didn't the judge care about Brian force-feeding Jimmy or making Jimmy cry when he dropped him off at preschool? Didn't he see that this is part of a pattern, that Brian abused her and is now abusing her children? How could the judge just dismiss all that as "water under the bridge"? Now she's spent all this money on her lawyer for this useless trial, her resources are depleted, and she's significantly worse off than before, with Brian having the children for five overnights in every two-week cycle.

I understand Beth's frustration. The outcome of this case, however, is not about protecting abusers or about not believing kids. This case goes to the heart of the way our adversarial system functions. In large part, it's about the rules of evidence. Specifically, about the rule against the admission of hearsay. Think about Brian's side, where I have stood many times before. Suppose, for a moment, that Beth had totally fabricated this story because she is so angry at Brian. Or that Beth (innocently) misunderstood what Jimmy was telling her. Or that Jimmy was unconsciously playing both sides of the fence, or fingered his father because at some level he knew that's what his mother wanted to hear. All those scenarios are possible, and if the statement can't be tested by asking Jimmy questions, how can a court distinguish between those versions and the version Beth would have presented, in which Jimmy was accurately reporting an event?

Imagine being a parent whose ability to see your child can be taken away merely by the other parent—a person who may have a motive to hurt you—saying that your child told her that you did something bad. No medical or other corroboration, nothing but your estranged spouse's testimony about a conversation she supposedly had with your child, which no one else heard. The potential for abuse is terrifying. The rule against the admission of hearsay is a cornerstone of our legal system for good reason. It safeguards us from the secondhand accusations of others.

So how do we protect Jimmy? Either way, it's bad for him. If Brian didn't injure Jimmy but the court believes that he did and suspends contact between them, Jimmy suffers from the loss of his father and the possibility of long-term, maybe even irreparable, damage to their relationship. If Brian did injure Jimmy but the court believes he didn't, Jimmy is at risk of being hurt again during future visits. There's no perfect solution.

I don't know what to think about Kaitlyn's testimony. Over the past week, I've gone back and forth. On the one hand, how could it be that she came to court bursting to tell a story she had told no one before, and one that so perfectly dovetailed with Jimmy's? On the other hand, if Beth had coached her, wouldn't she have tried to get Kaitlyn to take the narrative all the way through to seeing Brian squeeze Jimmy's arm? Why stop at Jimmy's saying his dad was hurting him? I don't know and I never will.

Now it's time to do damage control. Brian didn't get exactly what he asked for, but I'm sure he and Francis view this as a big win. He beat the abuse rap and has the kids four nights in a row every other week. Maybe, I will tell Beth, it'll work out okay. Maybe he'll control himself better with the kids now that he sees how close he came to losing them for what could have been a substantial period of time. Or maybe it will be worse, and they'll tell you about it and this time they will both be willing to tell other people as well. Custody orders can always be modified. All we have to allege to get into court is that the existing order is no longer in the best interests of the children. If we go back to Judge Diamond with additional evidence about Brian's harsh parenting, he could realize he got it wrong the first time and be unwilling to give Brian the benefit of the doubt a second time around. I'll advise Beth to keep a careful log of how the kids seem when they come back from Brian's, what they tell her, whether they're tired or hungry or sick, whether Kaitlyn's homework doesn't get turned in or her test scores suffer, whether either child consistently arrives at school late. This custody arrangement will give us a track record over a longer period to see how Brian is doing, I will tell her. We'll get useful information: Either it will give us evidence against him that could be the basis of a petition to reduce his custodial time, or it will show that the kids are doing fine, that he's a good enough parent, that he's holding it together, which is, after all, what she wants, right?

I don't expect to be able to talk to Beth about any of this yet. We're out in the hallway and she's crying. It's so unfair, she's saying, the system is so unfair. I do agree that if Brian did all the things Beth says he did, Jimmy and Kaitlyn are at risk of being hurt by him in the future, and my mother's heart goes out to Beth. But my lawyer's head does not agree that the system is unfair. Maybe I'm just too steeped in its culture to think otherwise. But I have a deep and abiding faith in the rules of evidence. I don't know what happened between Brian and Jimmy. I do know that I can plan our strategy going forward and think about how to explain it to Beth when she's ready to listen and absorb it. This trial is finished. And to quote Judge Diamond, it's time to move on.

Working Women

I am obsessed with the topic of women's economic self-sufficiency. In my early twenties, I thought it was important, as an abstract principle, for women to be able to support themselves. Decades later, after thousands of billable hours spent representing women rendered desperate and distraught by the prospect of divorce because of their total economic dependence on husbands, there's nothing abstract about it. I've been up close and personal with the ugly reality. What surprises me is whom it affects. I expect this kind of dependence with women older than I am, those who embraced a traditional homemaker role at a time when other options weren't on the table. Or with women who have not had educational opportunities. I continue to be puzzled by the large number of women my age and younger, women who were raised with the expectation that they would have careers, women with college or graduate school degrees, who quickly left or never entered the workforce and find themselves at age forty or fifty with no skills with which to earn a living.

Here's a composite client profile. Cathy meets Rick in law school. They fall in love and marry right after graduation. Both of them take and pass the bar exam and begin working at law firms. They buy a condo in the city and start a family. Cathy gives birth to a little girl, takes her allotted three-month maternity leave, goes back to the firm, finds the twelve-hour workdays totally unacceptable, and decides, with Rick's blessing, to leave. The plan is that after their daughter is in preschool, she will go back to work at a job with hours more compatible with parenthood.

Cathy loves being at home with the baby. She meets other stay-at-home moms and becomes involved in neighborhood activities. Rick likes having her at home, too. It relieves him of responsibility for most of the housework and errands and he can focus on their daughter in the evenings and on weekends. Money is tight, but he is making just enough to support their small family and this seems to be the best arrangement for all three of them. When the baby is two, Cathy looks into various job prospects, but it doesn't really make sense, given that they are planning to have a second child soon. They postpone her return to work.

By the time their second daughter is born, Rick's earnings are rising and he is on track for a partnership. He is also working longer hours. Cathy is completely absorbed by caring for a new baby and a three-year-old. Her brief career as a lawyer is receding into the background, crowded out by the demands of breastfeeding and preschool schedules and mothers' groups and piles of laundry.

Rick makes partner. With their older daughter now approaching kindergarten age, Cathy and Rick decide to move to a suburb with an excellent public school system. Real estate prices are high, but based on Rick's income, they are able to qualify for a large mortgage. When their older daughter enters kindergarten, Cathy meets a whole new group of stay-at-home moms and starts volunteering at school. Many of their new friends have three kids. Cathy and Rick had planned on having only two, but they love being parents, and the financial impact of a third child doesn't seem that great—school is free, and the house has plenty of space.

Now they have a little boy. Given that Cathy has been a full-time mom to their daughters, there is no question that she will do the same for their son, at least for the early years.

Life takes a lot of managing. The girls are involved in sports and ballet and music lessons; the baby has asthma, which requires numerous doctors' visits and medications and general monitoring of his health. Cathy, who had practiced law for two years, has now been at home raising children for eight years. She thinks again about returning to work, but it seems pointless. They'd have to hire a full-time nanny to care for the kids and the cost of that feels extravagant, even foolish, given the amount she anticipates earning. The commute into the city would make her workday very long. And, fundamentally, Cathy feels insecure about her legal skills. She is uncertain that anyone would hire her, given her lack of experience and long absence from the workplace. She and Rick discuss, he agrees, and they decide to postpone the decision until all three kids are in school full-time.

You can see where this is going. Cathy's decisions were all reasonable in the context of her life at the time. If she stays married to Rick, the only casualty will be her professional ambitions, but she might be able to pick those up again after fifteen or twenty years and slowly build her way into a satisfying career, especially since she won't be under any financial pressure because Rick would provide the real income for the family; hers would just be extra. None of this accounts for the cataclysm of divorce, looming like a storm cloud in their future.

Despite my concern about educated women giving up their careers, I am aware that it could have easily happened to me, had economic circumstances been different. Zoe was born when I had been practicing law for only a year and Alan was in graduate school. I thought it would be a snap: have a baby, take three months off, put that baby in day care, and head right back to the office. A brief interruption in the upward trajectory of my legal career. As ridiculous as this sounds, this is really how I saw the world at the time. My ignorance about the complexity of motherhood was breathtaking.

Everything started out as planned. I arranged to take a three-month maternity leave, cleaned off my desk, went into labor, and had my baby. After that, it all went out the window. I found my infant daughter intoxicating. The delicious smell of her fuzzy head made my eyes tear up. I couldn't stand to be separated from her for more than an hour or two. I loved being at home with her. (It might have helped that she rarely cried and slept like an angel.) I grew close to two women I had met during my pregnancy, both of whom had their first babies around the same time I did. We all lived in the same neighborhood on the Upper West Side of Manhattan and spent long afternoons in one another's apartments, nursing our babies, eating, chatting, and generally reveling in our new status as moms.

Between us, there was one big difference, however. I had to go back to work when Zoe was three months old and they did not. Wendy was taking an undefined amount of time off. She had quit her job and wasn't returning. Sarah was a singer and a songwriter and her work was pretty self-directed. Both were a few years older than I and both had planned carefully so they wouldn't have to work for a while. Not me. The end of my maternity leave was bearing down on me like a runaway train.

The culture we created in our little group fueled my fear

and anxiety about returning to work, but I didn't have a choice. Alan had worked as a carpenter to put me through law school, and now it was his turn. He was in the middle of architecture school. Fair is fair. I went through the incredibly painful process of finding someone to care for my precious Zoe (no day care for Wendy's and Sarah's kids!) and went back to the small firm where I had started working right out of law school. I packed my breast pump into my briefcase and wept every morning on the bus on the way to work. I was miserable. I wanted nothing more than to be back in that cocoon of new motherhood, sitting on the carpet in Wendy's lovely living room high above West End Avenue, drinking tea and discussing our babies' first signs of teething. I still hung out with Wendy and Sarah when I wasn't working, but it was as though I had moved to a foreign country. They were supportive and curious and a bit horrified. I think—actually, I know—they pitied me. Comparing myself with them, there was no question about my inadequacy as a mother.

Suppose I hadn't been married to a student. Or suppose that two years later, I hadn't been married to a new architect whose earnings were significantly lower than mine. Suppose, in other words, I had not been the primary breadwinner for my family at that time. If my husband had been, say, a doctor or a corporate lawyer or a finance guy, would I have breathed a sigh of relief and quit my job? I think not, but I can't say for sure. The pull of new motherhood was so strong, the cozy domesticity such a welcome shelter from the competitive, harsh world outside, the flood of emotion at the sight of my daughter's chubby hands and feet so powerful and delightful. I can imagine making the choice to stay in that sheltered world if I had the chance.

But it's dangerous. Back to Cathy and Rick. They grow apart. Their worlds are increasingly separate. He is operating in the public sphere at a high-powered job in the city. He's thinking about complex legal issues, deals he's involved in, cases he has to try. He's navigating the land mines of office politics. He doesn't really understand what Cathy does during the day, especially now that the kids are all in school. Cathy lives in the private sphere. She runs the household and makes sure everyone is fed, clothed, and taken where they need to go. She's interested in the kids' school and their activities; she's involved in building a new community playground, she's doing volunteer legal work for the local animal shelter. The world Rick moves in seems increasingly distant. She can talk to him about his cases, but how much he cares about them annoys her. He's disconnected from the day-to-day world she inhabits with the kids. Rick meets someone at work and has an affair. When Cathy finds out about it, she's upset but wants them to stay together. They go to counseling. It doesn't help. Rick feels that they've just grown too far apart. He moves out and files for divorce.

This is where I enter the picture. Cathy is now forty-two

and has been out of the job market for fifteen years. Despite the fact that she's a lawyer—a fact that Rick's lawyer will be sure to mention frequently—she has very limited work experience and from so long ago that it might be difficult to translate into a current job practicing law. After taxes, Rick brings home about $12,000 per month. All that money gets spent—their monthly mortgage payment alone is $4,000. They have a checking account, no savings to speak of, and Rick's 401(k), which they can't touch. The house has no equity in it, so selling it won't generate any cash.

Rick's income now has to be spread over two households. If Cathy stays in the house, the monthly amount of support Rick will have to pay her will cover the mortgage, utilities, and the payment on the minivan. Cathy will have nothing left over to buy groceries or clothes, much less for ballet and horseback riding lessons. What is she going to do? How is she going to live? They can sell the house and she can rent an apartment, but apartments are expensive in their neighborhood and she'll need to stay there to keep the kids in their current school, since she doesn't want to uproot them—dealing with the divorce is bad enough. Despite the affair and their emotional distance, Cathy would absolutely choose to stay in the marriage rather than turn her and the kids' lives upside down. But she doesn't have the power to make that choice. If Rick wants a divorce, it will happen.

Step back and think about what this does to the emotional playing field. How can Cathy navigate the difficulties of an unhappy marriage when it's all intertwined with a sickening fear of having her electricity shut off? And she at least has an advanced degree and a license to practice a relatively lucrative profession. Suppose she had only a B.A. in English, now twenty years stale, or no degree at all, and no work history other than waitressing? She would be lucky to land a job at Starbucks.

Now imagine that Cathy's life took a different path. Suppose she had gone back to work when her kids were young. Even if she had worked part-time for a while and even if she chose to leave the firm with the ridiculously high billable-hour requirement in favor of a more flexible (and probably lower-paying) job, after seventeen years of practicing law, Cathy would be capable of supporting herself and the kids, and she would be able to think about divorce entirely differently. Here's what she'd be examining: Does she still love Rick? Can she tolerate his having had an affair? Would it be better for the children, on balance, if they stayed together or split? And if he chooses to pursue a divorce despite her desire to stay together, she would figure out how to cope. She might be unhappy, but she'd be weighing unhappy choices, feeling in control of her destiny even if displeased with her options.

Instead, she is staring into an abyss where the life she created for herself and her family is about to come to an abrupt end.

There is no question that money is power, and the power

dynamic in marriages where one person is financially dependent on the other is dramatically different from that in marriages where both spouses are capable of paying the bills.

I COME TO this issue not only as a lawyer representing clients but also as an employer of young moms, a role in which I seem to specialize. How do you set up a workplace where women don't feel so pressured to choose between career and motherhood? From the get-go, Joni and I tried hard to build a firm that supports women lawyers. We wanted to be able to practice our profession successfully and have time to raise our children. That's the engine that drove Joni to leave the big law firm and hang her own shingle, and me to look for part-time employment when my kids were young. We don't want women lawyers to feel compelled to make the choice Cathy made; we want them to be able to work and develop professionally and earn money and also be hands-on parents.

When our first associate announced her pregnancy, we realized we needed a maternity-leave policy. We had to balance what we thought was right versus what we could afford. Our revenue is generated by attorneys billing their time; an attorney who is not working, but is being paid, is a significant financial drain on the firm. We came up with this policy:

"You can take at least three months off for birth or adoption of a child. We will pay you for the first six weeks of your leave, and you can add your accumulated PTO [paid time off] to that if you wish. We will keep your health insurance in effect during the three-month period, at our expense. Assuming that we can accommodate you—and we will make every effort to do so—you can take more time off, which may or may not include our continuing to pay for your health insurance, by prior arrangement with us. If you want to come back to work part-time, with proportionally reduced salary and benefits, we will also make every effort to accommodate you."

Seems simple enough. By European standards, paying someone for six weeks (generally more, because of vacation time being added to the leave) and giving them three months off seems stingy. By U.S. standards for small business, we discovered, it's considered generous. Really didn't seem like a big deal to us. Until, that is, the perfect pregnancy storm occurred when everyone had babies in succession. Lisa, Kristine, Stephanie, and Megan—it was one after the other, falling like dominoes.

There was a solid year when at least one lawyer was out on maternity leave, leaving Joni and me (and Megan, when she was not having a baby herself) listening to the constant sucking sound of money rushing out the door to pay attorneys who were not in the office and billing clients. We're small, only six lawyers. We practice family law, not mergers and acquisitions, and our profit margin is far lower than in other areas of the legal profession. It was tough.

Some nights during that Year of the Maternity Leave, I would be working late, seeing the sky grow dark and the building cleaning staff arrive, missing dinner with my family, and I would think about how I was there at 8 p.m., earning money to pay another woman so she could be at home with her baby. I want to say I felt proud of that choice, but I would be less than truthful if I didn't admit that I often felt resentful. Payroll comes every two weeks like the tide. You can't stop it. If you don't have the money to meet it, you don't pay yourself. If you still don't have enough money, you have to borrow it. During this period we did both those things. It was challenging to confront the sharp edge where the values we wanted to embody in our workplace, the culture we sought so hard to create, met my inner capitalist, who was whispering, "Exactly why are you doing this? Nobody paid you for maternity leave! You have college tuition to pay!" And we couldn't very well tell our associates that our maternity-leave policy applied only if they staggered their pregnancies to cause the least damage to our cash flow. Believe me, though, we thought about it. At a very basic level, for me to give one of my employees more time to spend with her family, I have to spend less time with mine.

These are all tough choices. But they are choices I can make in a considered way; I can factor in those college tuition bills, I can think about my commitments at home, and I can figure out how much of that trade-off I'm willing to make. That kind of thinking, that kind of control over one's destiny (within limits, obviously), is exactly what Cathy does not have. She is at the mercy of Rick's decision-making. For women who have had the good fortune and perseverance to get education and training that enable them to work at a job that can support a family, it is a serious gamble to put those skills aside in favor of being cared for by a husband. It might feel all cozy and comfortable, but there's no guarantee of happily ever after. The fairy tale can end in a heartbeat.

Closing Argument

There's a courthouse saying that criminal lawyers see bad people at their best and family lawyers see good people at their worst. We deal with people who are raw, who are hurting. They tell us about what happens behind closed doors, about jealousy and anguish, about drug abuse and violence, about illness and depression. And we come to know them, fast.

Some of the people we work with are so stunningly absorbed by their own misery that they cannot see straight. They lash out, they're vindictive, they hurt even the ones they love. That's the good people at their worst. But there's also a flip side. There are plenty of people who, in the midst of crisis, inspire awe with their strength and sound judgment. I have watched with pure admiration as a client sucks up his legitimate fury at his extremely badly behaving ex-wife because he knows it would be best for his kids if he told them nothing but how much fun they're going to have at Mommy's. I have applauded the grit and dignity of a client who, at the age of forty-nine, having not worked for twenty years, goes out and finds an entry-level job at a clothing store paying just above the minimum wage because she knows she cannot live off her alimony. She's ready and willing to make a new life for herself, without complaint. And I often wonder, if I stood in my clients' shoes, would I be capable of such decency and bravery? Or would I be unable to see past the pain?

This is the personal side of the practice of family law. It's Darlene's grief over the judge's removing her baby from her custody and Susan's joy in being able to relocate with her children. It's Eddie's bitter experience of betrayal when Marco failed to live up to his promises and Mary's stubborn insistence on retaining a painting as a singular emblem of security and familiarity when her long marriage ended. It's Ann and Paula and Michael's excitement about creating a child together.

But these cases also represent a substantive legal side, a body of law that is changing at a dizzying pace. From the time my older daughter took her first wobbly steps to the day we helped lug her more-than-distressed furniture up three flights of stairs to her tiny apartment in Brooklyn—the short span of a single generation—the transformation of society through legislation and judicial decisions, and the cultural trends that sometimes push the law forward and other times lag behind it, has been breathtaking.

Like same-sex marriage. Twenty-five years ago it wasn't even a glint in the public's eye. Today, in a *People* magazine feature called "Fun with the Family," Elton John, his husband, and their two-year-old son, and Neil Patrick Harris, his partner, and their young twins, wave happily from the deck of an elegant boat in St. Tropez. "All aboard!" the caption proclaims. "It's a daddy's reunion." Polls now show that a majority of Americans think same-sex marriage should be legal, up from a little over a third of the population just six years earlier. In the last two years, the number of states that permit gay couples to marry increased by fifty percent.

Or joint custody. In the past, custody was rarely awarded to fathers and truly shared parenting was unusual. Within the last three decades, gender roles have shifted dramatically within the family, as more women enter the workforce and men take on greater child-rearing responsibilities. Those trends, combined with new studies in child development and organized advocacy by fathers' rights groups, who objected to having their parental roles marginalized after divorce, have remade the law. Currently, all fifty states have laws that provide for or promote shared custody. There used to be a stigma associated with being a mother whose children didn't reside primarily with her, and many of my women clients whose husbands wanted shared custody were adamantly opposed to it on principle. In my practice today, many, if not most, of the mothers I represent are comfortable with sharing custody. In fact, they often expect and welcome it.

Alternative ways to create children through assisted reproductive technology are becoming widely available and commonly used. The rights of transgendered people are being recognized. There is a broad consensus about the problem of domestic violence, with laws against it in every state, and at the federal level through the Violence Against Women Act, that provide civil protection for survivors. The explosion of lawsuits brought by victims of child sexual abuse has exposed the most horrifying of family secrets to the bright light of the courtroom. And the list goes on.

Layered over this shifting legal terrain are social changes that affect the way we practice family law. One is the disintegration of personal privacy. Trails of information, following us like Hansel and Gretel's breadcrumbs, drop from our laptops, our cell phones, and our Facebook accounts. The ability to stalk one's ex through GPS and stealth text and computer technologies brings new challenges to what might otherwise be a run-of-the-mill divorce. Another is the emergence of new ideas about how to address family disputes. Just like the movement a generation ago to de-medicalize childbirth, there is a strong and growing interest in personally taking charge of the process, in removing such disputes from the courts, to mediate, to collaborate, to handle them without lawyers. The do-it-yourself generation wants to take care of its divorces, just as it wants to grow its own vegetables. There is now the notion of the "good divorce," along with the concept that you can still be a family postdivorce, just a reconfigured one; that you can celebrate holidays together and be friends with each other's new spouses, that divorce doesn't have to be war, and that it may even be worthy of marking as a life-cycle event with the ritual of a ceremony.

But no matter how the law and the practice evolve, driving it all will still be the powerful engine of human emotion. That will stay the same as long as Darlene and Susan and Eddie and Mary and Ann and Paula and Michael continue to form intimate relationships, whether those relationships take place in cyberspace, through telepathy, or even on different planets. The details will change, but the essentials will not. And we family lawyers will be there, advising, advocating, and negotiating the timeless passions of the human heart.

ACKNOWLEDGMENTS

Not every aspiring author is fortunate enough to have a relent-
lessly dedicated mentor, but I was. Shortly after my first foray
into nonlegal writing by way of a blog about practicing family law, my close friend, the author and investigative journalist
Cathryn Jakobson Ramin, read my initial posts, told me emphatically that "this should be a book," and we were off and
running. Her constant encouragement, combined with sometimes brutal editing (including her frequent admonishments
to "stop writing like a lawyer") were invaluable. I had never
heard of a book proposal before Cathryn insisted I write one,
promptly read it, ripped it apart, and made me do it all over
again. Without her commitment to this project and her generos-
ity in sharing both time and her extensive expertise, there would
be no book. Cath, from the bottom of my heart, I thank you.

I also wish to thank Carol Schneider at Workman Publishing
for making the introduction to Elisabeth Scharlatt, publisher
of Algonquin Books, and to Elisabeth for taking a chance on
me. And I am especially grateful for the time and attention I've
received from my editor, the wonderful Amy Gash, who pa-
tiently advised and revised, debated issues from legal substance

to individual word choice, and always made me feel like a real author, not just a lawyer masquerading as one.

My first readers and my consistent champions throughout this process have been my husband, Alan Metcalfe, and my daughters, Zoe Metcalfe-Klaw and Robin Metcalfe-Klaw. The three of you are my world and I adore you. I also want to thank my second circle of readers and advisers, the women whose love and support I rely on in all endeavors, my sisters, Joanna Schultz, Susan Klaw, and Rebecca Klaw, and my mother-in-law, Ann Breen Metcalfe. And I will be forever indebted to my law partners, Joni Berner and Megan Watson, as well as our firm administrator, Judy Stouffer, for encouraging me to undertake this venture, for supporting my "writing Fridays," and for never once asking why I wasn't in the office billing clients.

Finally, to my clients: thank you. Your lives have intersected with mine in intense bursts of intimacy. You have confided in me about your desires and your fears; you have trusted me to be your advocate in disputes about that which matters most to us all—our families. It is your stories, details changed but essence remaining, that make up this book. It's a privilege to share them.